Jake,

Thank you
for your support

Steve
Davis

Copyright © 2022 by Steven Paris

All rights reserved. No part of this book may be used or reproduced in any manner whatsoever without written permission from the author, except in the case of brief quotations embodied in literary articles or reviews.

For permissions or requests please contact the author at:

steveparisbook@gmail.com

ISBN: 9798371612250
Imprint: Independently published

Author photo credit: Channing Devane Trick
Cover photo/design: Steven Paris

FORWARD

Many people look fondly upon their childhood. People usually remember their parents as people they were able to count on through anything. They remember holidays, birthdays, family time, school events, and so many other times that make everyone warm and fuzzy inside.

Many look fondly on their friendships and feel the same way. That has become the norm we all abide by. It's hard to imagine your life not being that way. I know, I, for one, often look upon my childhood as stable, loving, engaging, and fun.

But what happens when that is not your reality? It can make someone bitter, angry, and dangerous. Not in Steve's case. He is the exception to the expectation. He has decided to make his life one of meaning, love, giving back, and philanthropy. His story is proof that your beginnings don't need to match your endings, and that things and events you think will break you- will in fact build you up to greater things.

I always equate Steve with a glow stick. People tried to crack him, and instead of breaking, he has been glowing for decades. He is an inspiration to everyone he meets, and this harrowing story of his beginnings will make you realize that you can be anything you dream- regardless of where you started. This is the story of a hero to so many- one who doesn't need a cape.

-Melissa P. Bernal, M.A.

"For the men and women who never got to be children, and for the children who never got to feel love."

-Michael K. Williams

THE BEGINNING OF THE END OF MY CHILDHOOD
JUNE 1986

As the car approached the long, steep driveway, I was suddenly overcome by panic. I had never had much of a normal family life before. But now as the new foster home approached larger than life through the windshield, I realized for the first time that I was an orphan. Maybe not in the traditional sense of the word, but being given up by my father to live with some family was all I needed to be convinced that I was not wanted.

Life hadn't been very easy for me in the past few years. I had already experienced homelessness, being stuck in the middle of a divorce, and taking care of myself for days at a time. Now, as I was approaching eleven years old, I was headed for a whole new playing field. A whole new game where I was the mascot, and the other team was kicking the shit out of me every chance they got.

The Division of Youth and Family Services (DYFS), had been called at my father's request. He wanted me placed in a new home. He had told them that he would no longer take care of me. Opting instead to start a new life with his new fiancee, Nikki, She was like my sworn enemy. A woman that I couldn't even try to like or respect.

   Since my own mother was unable or apparently unwilling to take me, DYFS stepped in. Placing me at the starting line of what would be a race that would go on for more than two decades. A race that would lead me through each and every facet of the juvenile system, while preparing me for my inevitable transition into the adult criminal justice system. A race that I am still running today.

HILLSIDE, NJ
1982

When I was six years old, and a relatively normal child living a somewhat average life, my parents separated. Having been close to my father, I was both crushed and very confused by this. I did the normal thing that most kids do at that age in that situation. I blamed myself. In my own mind, it was my fault that my parents weren't staying together. First, I cried, then I moped, and then the drama began. I started to act out in every way that I could. Sometimes I refused to go to school. Sometimes, I went, and sometimes (usually most of the time) I tried to drive all of my teachers nuts. This would include fighting with the other kids and even throwing things at the teachers themselves, I would throw anything… books, chairs, even the desks. It didn't matter. I made it my own personal mission to ensure that everyone around me was given a hard time. I wanted to make everyone feel my pain. I wanted them to hurt. After all, I was hurting, wasn't I? Why shouldn't everyone else around me suffer? That was my outlook on life. A pretty crappy outlook to have at six years old, but it made sense to me.

My acting out was not limited to school. Now, decades years later, I realize that my behavior at home was much worse than it was at school. My sister got the brunt of it. I used to kick her, punch her, and bite her like I was a vampire and she was the last source of blood on the planet. Throwing TV sets down flights of stairs became the norm for me. My younger brother was spared from my rage, He was only three years old at the time. I really didn't have any real angst toward him. Actually, I kind of felt bad for him because deep down I knew he would probably have it worse than I had it.

I acted out because I wanted my father back. After about a year of trying to torture my dissected family, I got what I wanted. My mother decided that I should be granted my wish. She packed up my stuff and drove me to my father's apartment in Bayonne, New Jersey. I felt liberated from an evil empire. I figured that the end of all of my problems was right around the bend. I would wind up being totally wrong in my calculations.

BAYONNE, NJ
1982

My dad welcomed me with open arms. Our relationship became more like a friendship rather than a normal father-son bond. Sure, he would still lay down the law when I was misbehaving but for the majority of the time, I had it pretty good.

Dad was a mailman working a route that he had held for about 13 years. He used to take me out to walk his route with him during the summer months. I liked that because most of the old ladies that he would deliver to would give me pieces of candy or a few spare quarters. As a kid with a pocketful of quarters, I felt like I was on top of the world. By the end of the week, I could buy so many pieces of penny candy from the corner store that I could barely carry them home by myself. During the days that I walked with my dad, we always had lunch at this little bar on Kennedy Boulevard called EJ's. EJ's was a few blocks up from the apartment that we lived in, so most of the patrons were local idiots and drunks. Dad would sit at the bar drinking his beer, and I would sit next to him and eat pizza. I could have myself a bottle of Coke, dad would have his bottle of beer. I could play pinball or PAC MAN. Dad could shoot darts. Once in a while, we'd shoot pool together. He walked me through all of the intricacies of the game.

I was content. It made me feel important to be able to hang out at a bar. The owner even kept a pair of my roller skates under the bar for me to use when I wanted to go out front and skate. Through my eyes at the time, there didn't seem to be anything wrong with a father and his seven-year-old kid hanging out in a bar together. Obviously, I see now that my dad was no different than the schmucks sitting at the bar with him. He was also a drunk. It took me a lot of years to come to that realization.

After about two years of living together in Bayonne, my dad told me that we were moving to California. He said that he was quitting his job at the Post Office and we were getting on a plane to go to San Diego to live by the beach. I was ecstatic! California!! Wow! I was beside myself. I pictured surfing, sun, no more crappy snow-ridden winters. I felt like the coolest kid on the block. Telling everyone who would listen.

"I'm moving to California, you are going to be stuck here in the freezing cold every winter."

This could often lead to little spats and fights, but I didn't care. Dad taught me to defend myself, so I had no problem beating up on the neighborhood kids. Actually, I became quite good at it. Fighting would eventually become a way for me to settle all of my problems.

SAN DIEGO, CA
1984

I had about a month left of third grade when we got on the plane. With a short layover in Chicago, we were landing in San Diego by 1pm. We were met at the airport by my dad's sister Patty. A woman that I had never met, and didn't know existed until a few weeks before. Patty had two kids, my cousins Peyton who was about five years older than me, and Paul who had me by one year. The plan was for us to stay with her until we got on our feet.

My newfound relatives lived on the fourth floor of a seven-story apartment complex on La Jolla Boulevard just two blocks from the ocean. The first few nights in my new surroundings were a bit weird for me due to the time difference between coasts   However, I adjusted rather fast.

Since the schooling systems were different on the west coast, I didn't have to finish the remainder of the third grade. I pretty much just hung around the house during the day. When Paul came home we would go to the beach and go body surfing or boogie boarding. Sometimes we would climb the cliffs that overlooked Pacific Beach. Life was grand. This was a whole new adventure for me. The fast differences between San Diego and Jersey were like the differences between Heaven and Hell. Paul introduced me to the local kids, and soon they became my friends as well. At first, some of them were a bit shocked by my "Joisey" accent, but after a few months, the accent started to dissipate. I started to become a genuine California kid. I had a dark tan. I went everywhere without wearing shoes. I started to learn how to skateboard. I even took up surfing! I wound up fitting in well with the lifestyle that California had to offer.

In the midst of the New Wave generation of music, I was addicted to MTV. When I left Jersey I was a huge Michael Jackson fan. Now it was all about Duran Duran. My cousins and I would stage little performances for our parents. All in all, I was a happy kid. Sure I missed some of my friends and my family back home, but the sun-filled days and the crisp Pacific had a strange way of making all of that drift away. Before I knew it I felt like I had lived out there all of my life. With the exception of my slight accent which had come and gone at times, most of the people that I met couldn't tell the difference between me and any of the other local kids. Little did I know that all that would change very soon. The new life that I had begun and started to love so much soon would come crashing down on me like one of the waves that I spent so much time watching from the cliffs in La Jolla.

After a few months of living with Aunt Patty, Dad and I got ourselves a little duplex apartment on Bayard Street. It wasn't very big, but it was home. Dad had a new job as a salesman for a marketing company. And I was enjoying my first summer in my new digs. I didn't hang out that much with my cousin Paul. He only lived a few blocks away, but I felt the need to seek out my own new friends rather than having to rely on his. Most of my days were spent riding my bike around the neighborhood trying to keep myself busy until my dad came home and we could hang out. That was the best thing about my life with my dad. We would actually hang out. It was like we were buddies. Even though I was way too young at the time, he would let me have a beer to drink every now and then. In fact, the first time that I ever got drunk was at a graduation party for my dad's girlfriend, Phyllis's son when we were still living in Bayonne. Shit, the first time that I ever smoked pot was out of his personal stash. He didn't know it, but I used to pinch his stash every once in a while and smoke a joint with my friends.

We would take long rides up the coast, going to San Francisco for a weekend here and there. We'd drive up to spend the day at Disneyland, dad wanted to show me the world. At least a small part of it. I was like an eager schoolboy, and he was my teacher. Gone were the days of running around the projects in Bayonne. We were reborn. Belonging to a much better class than before.

"There's No Life East of I-5!!" That was what the bumper sticker said on the back of our 1978 Toyota Corolla hatchback. That was our mantra. Pretty soon I didn't give a shit about anything back in Jersey. I had very limited contact with my mother or my siblings. And it didn't bother me at all. Our duplex was a side-by-side unit. There was a couple named John and Larissa who moved in next door to us. They became like an extended family to us. I had the hots for Larissa really bad. I think she knew it too. I started to spend a lot of time next door. Especially during the day when my dad and John were working. Larissa didn't seem to mind one bit. She didn't work, so she'd hang around the apartment half-dressed most of the time. She made little attempt to cover herself up just for my sake. There were many days when all she had on was a long T-Shirt. Nothing underneath, no bra, no panties, Just that T-shirt. I would often catch a view of her naked crotch while she was curled up on the sofa watching TV. To this day I am still not sure if she knew that I was looking and enjoying the view, or if she was just a free-spirited California girl who was oblivious to that sort of thing. Either way was fine for me at the time. Once in a while, she would pull out some weed and smoke a little. I never let on that I knew what she was actually doing, and after a while, she started to offer me some. We agreed that my dad couldn't find out, and we would spend lazy afternoons getting high and watching TV. Naked crotch shots, weed to smoke, and pleasant company, what else does a growing boy need ??

Soon summer was over and I started the fourth grade at Bird Rock Elementary School. This place was like no school that I had ever seen. The schools that I had attended thus far were huge four and five-story brick monstrosities that would stretch for 4 square blocks. Bird Rock was built on a huge grassy knoll, and unlike others, I had known, was only one floor. There were no hallways. The only thing that was indoors was the classrooms and the cafeteria. There wasn't even a gym. The gym class was held outside due to the constant beautiful weather. The teachers were mostly pleasant and I was actually participating in class. My cousin Paul was in the class just two doors up from mine, and we would have lunch together. Most of my fellow students were rich kids because the school district was actually in La Jolla which was a pretty wealthy area. I myself lived right on the edge of the Pacific Beach area, so I got to go to a better school that some kids say, ten blocks south of my house. I wasn't the only non-rich kid in the school, but I definitely started to gravitate toward the rich kids. As I made new friends I was astounded by the way these kids lived. Most of their houses could hold my duplex within them five or six times. Is this what I could expect to be surrounded by for the rest of my years?? I sure hoped so. My new friends didn't seem to care that I didn't have money. They knew right away that I was not born locally. Again, my ever-present accent gave me away. I think that this intrigued them. To them, I was kind of an exotic being. I am sure that most of them traveled before, but not to Jersey.

As the beginning of 1985 approached, I had settled into a fairly normal routine. I'd go to school then I would hang out with my friends afterward. I took an active approach to my education. I was enjoying learning. I was no longer acting out in class. I had stopped throwing things at my teachers. I was an all-around normal child.

Then came Troy, who was a bully. Troy was in the sixth grade. Everybody in school knew who Troy was. Most of the kids tried to street clear of him to avoid a problem. I was one of them. I had already had a few minor run-ins with him in the past, so I knew how he was. But I also knew his type well. Kids like him were a dime-a-dozen back home. The kids that felt a need to try to bully the younger kids because it made them feel like they were almighty. These are the same kids that got beat up by their older brothers and their fathers regularly. They had something to prove to everyone else.

I don't quite remember exactly what started it, but I was shooting marbles, and before I knew it, Troy was trying to flex his bully muscles on me. As we began to scrap it out, he made the mistake of punching me on the top of my head. A mistake that caused his right hand to break in a few places. I felt the hit. I heard bones crack. At first, I thought the crack was my own head. Hearing Troy scream aloud in pain while curling his right arm to his stomach as he doubled over, assured me that it wasn't my head that was broken. It was his hand. In an instant, I knew what I had to do. I had to use this to my advantage to fix this kid once and for all. I started to hit him harder than I had ever hit anything before. When he dropped to the ground, I started to kick him with every ounce of energy that I had. The fight was broken up. Troy went to the nurse's office, me to the principal's office. I wound up getting suspended from school for ten days because of the fight. I also wound up gaining a bit of notoriety for beating the shit out of a bully who was not only two years my senior, but who was also twice my size.

I still had to go home and tell my dad that I was suspended from school. I figured that this would wind up with me getting quite an ass-whooping myself, so I approached the subject very delicately to my father. Much to my chagrin, he took the news well. He was mad though. Not at me for fighting and getting kicked out of school but for the school suspending me in the first place. He didn't agree that I should be in trouble for defending myself. I guess he never expected that self-defense was a problem in the schools out there. Back home I might have gotten detention for something like that. Surely I wouldn't have been suspended.

Dad told me that he was going to call the school and have the situation straightened out.

"No son of mine is going to be kicked out of school for defending himself!", he said to me as I looked up at him through awe-inspired eyes.

This man was my hero. Not only was he OK with the fact that I was once again viewed as a derelict by my school system, but he was standing up for what he had taught me. I didn't think in a million years that I wouldn't be getting the shit kicked out of me for getting suspended from school.

The next morning dad woke me up and told me that it was alright to go to school. I got out of bed, ate breakfast, and got on my bike to ride to school. As I walked into the classroom, my teacher, Mr. Whipple had an odd look on his face as he watched me take my assigned seat. After the rest of the students milled in and sat down, he approached my desk and asked me to step outside with him to have a word.

"What are you doing back here in school today Steven?" he asked quizzically. Before I had the chance to respond, he came back in a stern voice. "You're supposed to be serving your suspension for the next ten days!"

Confused, I looked up at him and responded, "My said that it was OK for me to come back to school. He said that he had straightened it out."

Mr. Whipple glanced over my shoulder at the principal who was approaching from behind me and said, "I am not sure what your father told your son, but you are not supposed to be here in school today. You are suspended!!" in a very loud tone of voice.

I looked at this guy like the idiot that I thought he was. Who the hell did he think he was telling me that I couldn't be at school?? My dad told me to go to school. Here I was, at school, and now I've got some moron telling me that I wasn't supposed to be there. What was I supposed to do?? I looked at my teacher and the principal and just blurted out,

"I'm not going anywhere, I have a right to an education and you can't deny me that right. My dad told me to come to school today so here I am. Daring him with my eyes I followed up with "Make me leave!"

That's when it happened Mr. Whipple grabbed my arm like a candy store owner would grab a kid he caught shoplifting. He tried to drag me down the walkway. Now, I had been in a similar situation with a teacher back home, and dad told me that if a teacher EVER put their hands on me in any way, I should kick him in the nuts, punch him in the gut, and run from school immediately! So that's exactly what I did. I spun around and kicked him as hard as I could in his nuts. When he let go of my arm, I punched him square in the gut.

I didn't stop running until I got home. I had totally forgotten about my bike which was changed up in the school parking lot. I just ran home. As I approached the house I saw Larissa sitting on the front porch in a bikini top and a pair of short shorts!! Normally I would have really enjoyed this, but now I was too concerned with what happened. She immediately saw the look of disdain on my face and stood up.

"Steven, what's wrong? Why are you running down the street screaming at nine o'clock in the morning? Shouldn't you be in school?" she asked with a concerned look on her face.

Not realizing that I was actually screaming as I ran, I tried to catch my breath, and between gasps, I panted,

"My teacher at school...grabbed me...and... tried to hurt me."

With the conviction of a mother fighting for the life of her child, Larissa screamed,

"What are you serious??"

She looked down at me like I was a bird that fell out of a nest and put both of her arms around me to console me.

"I am going to call your father, okay baby, you're safe here with me. We'll get to the bottom of this, don't worry. Come inside with me, you'll be okay."

Larissa grabbed my hand and walked me into the house to call my dad. Before she picked up the phone, she reached into the wooden box on the coffee table and pulled out her stash of weed. Holding it up in the air as if to ask me if I wanted to smoke some, she reached for the phone.

I looked at her and said, "I can't right now. Once you call my dad, he will probably come right home. There is no way that I can be stoned when he gets here."

She nodded and began to dial his work number. As she walked into the kitchen to talk, I looked down at the wooden box and figured, what the hell! I reached into the bag and pulled out a joint. Instead of smoking it then, I put it into my pocket so I would have it for later.

I could hear Larissa in the kitchen trying to explain in a raspy voice what had happened, but I could only pick up parts of the conversation. "He's here with me right now...ok...I will tell him Bob...ok...we'll be here...Bye!" Then she walked back into the living room, plopped down on the couch, and said to me, "Your Dad will be here in a little bit. I'm gonna smoke this, and fix us something to eat. Are you hungry, sweetie??" she asked ever so delicately.

I told her I probably should eat something and we walked into the kitchen. She was toking away on her joint as she made us a sandwich to split. I was ok now, I really wasn't too concerned about what I had done. Actually, I was more concerned about what my dad was going to do to my teacher once he got home.

About forty-five minutes later I could hear the Toyota screech into the driveway. Dad came bursting through the door with a look on his face that was a bit familiar to me. It was the same look he had when he was about to throw me a beating for something I did wrong. The only difference was that this Look was about five times the normal look. I knew that someone was going to get their ass kicked. I wondered at that very second if Mr. Whipple had any clue what he had gotten himself into. Did he know that he was about to have my dad's wrath thrown upon him? I seriously doubted it.

After explaining in full detail what happened to dad and Larissa, the three of us got in the car and sped toward Bird Rock Elementary. Without bothering to check in at the office, dad asked me to show him where my classroom was. As I guided him up the walkway. I could hear him grunting and breathing in and out very deeply. He was really pissed. We approached the classroom and Larissa held my hand firmly as my dad knocked on the classroom door. When the teacher came to answer the knock, dad punched him right in the mouth. The poor bastard didn't even know it was coming.

"Who the fuck do you think you are putting our hands on my kid, you stupid fuck!", he exclaimed as Mr. Whipple grabbed his face in agony.

"Wait...You don't understand.." Mr. Whipple pleaded as dad hit him again, "..I was only trying to escort him off.." WHAM!, another punch flew, cutting him off before he could finish his sentence.

Dad followed this up by pushing him to the ground and pointing down at him while he yelled about how to treat a child. Mr. Whipple was just laying there with blood dripping from his lip. His eyes were the same as a deer's are when staring down an eighteen-wheeler traveling at seventy miles an hour.

A few grunts and groans from Mr. Whipple trying to explain what happened was the last thing my dad wanted to hear at the time. He grabbed my left hand, Larissa grabbed my right, and he looked at me and asked,

"Are you ok Steven?" I nodded yes, "Ok, let's get out of here." we turned hand in hand and dad stopped, turned around, and pulled back his foot to kick my teacher,

"Never touch my son again! You got that?" he said, as Mr. Whipple curled up for the expected shot.

He didn't kick him though. As Mr. Whipple started to give his answer, dad just walked away. We walked right past the principal, and a few other teachers who were coming up the walkway to see what was going on. Back then, there weren't security guards posted in schools the way that there are now. If that same thing happened today, I probably would have been arrested for kicking my teacher, and my dad surely would have been for assaulting him. Nothing came of it though. Mr. Whipple didn't tell the principal exactly what happened. The cops weren't called. It went away very quietly. We did, however, get a phone call from the principal saying that they had decided that I was no longer under suspension for the fight that I had gotten into. But I was suspended for hitting my teacher. Dad took the new suspension with a grain of salt.

That night Dad, John, Larissa, and I all went out for dinner and ice cream at Farrell's. Ten days later, I went back to school. That teacher never gave me a problem again. In fact, he let me do pretty much what I wanted for the rest of the time that I attended his class.

A few months after my debacle with the teaching staff of Bird Rock Elementary, I had my first experience with the long arm of law enforcement. I wasn't the one who was in trouble though. It was my dad who was the culprit.

I woke up as I usually did on a school day. I took a shower, had breakfast, and was sitting in the living room watching TV when the front door shattered open. Before I knew it my house was swarming with men wearing blue windbreakers emblazoned with the words like "Postal Inspector" and "FBI" on them. They swept right past me and tackled my father. Some of them had their guns drawn. Some didn't. They really didn't seem to notice that there was a child sitting on the couch as they dragged my father through the living room toward the front door. As dad was being escorted in cuffs through the door, I could hear him yelling to me,

"Steven, don't worry! Go to your Aunt Patty's house and wait for me to call...I will take care of this! Just go to your aunt's."

He was going to take care of it. The cynic in me jumped out right at that moment. Take care of it. The same way he was gonna take care of my suspension? He never even called the school when he had told me that it was ok to return. Now, granted, that situation got worked out, but the fact that my dad was being dragged out of our house in handcuffs while yelling "I'll take care of it..." had me a bit skeptical at the time.

Nevertheless, I complied. I jumped on my bike and rode over to my aunt's apartment building. When I rang the doorbell I wondered what she was going to do when I told her that her brother was just dragged away by the FBI. She opened the door and invited me in just as she always did.

"Hey kiddo, what's up? Are you here to see Paulie? I'll go get him, come on in."

"Actually Aunt Patty, a bunch of men in blue windbreakers just dragged dad out of the house in handcuffs. He told me to come here and wait for him to call, so here I am"

I wasn't crying. I wasn't upset, I really wasn't all that shocked that it had happened at all. Sure, when they were bursting through the door I was a little scared. The only time I had seen something like that was in the movies. But given some of the things that I had already been through at my age, I really wasn't that surprised. My aunt though, she was a little more upset!

"What? Oh my goodness! Tell me what happened! Are you alright? Did they hurt you??" All of her questions were directed toward my well-being, not her brother's.

Apparently, she wasn't that surprised that her little brother was a criminal. I went inside and explained to her what had happened while we waited for the phone to ring. She cursed and ranted a bit about such a young child having to see something like that. Then she calmed down. I had settled in front of the TV and before we knew it, the sun was beginning to set.

Around six thirty the phone rang, and my aunt jumped to answer it.

"Hello...yes Bob, he's here..he's alright, What happened?" she inquired as she was pacing back and forth through the kitchen. "So what are you going to do? I can watch him if you want...hold on, here he is. "

I reached for the receiver and put it to my ear to talk to my dad, "Hello?"

"Steven, are you ok?" Dad asked nonchalantly, "I'm ok Dad, what happened? Are you coming home??"

"I will be home in a few days, I have some things that I have to take care of here", he said with a slight exhale,

"Do you want to stay there with your aunt, or would you rather stay at the house and have Larissa keep an eye on you for a few days?"

With a smirk on my face, I thought to myself "What the hell do you think Dad?"

"I would rather be home Dad. I don't want to stay here if I don't have to. I will be ok at home."

"Ok, fine son, you go home and I will be back in a few days. If you need anything just ask Larissa or John. Put your aunt back on the line."

"He wants to talk to you again", I said as I handed her the phone, and started to grab my things to leave. I wanted to get the hell out of there before she blew her lid.

"What do you mean he's going to go home? He is a nine-year-old child. I will take care of him....No....He cannot take care of himself..Bob, do you have any idea what you are doing to this kid?"

She ranted on like this for about five minutes before slamming down the phone with one last word, "Fine!" I looked up at her and could see that she didn't want me to leave, but I grabbed my stuff and walked out the door while she was fumbling around trying to grab her purse and catch me before I left.

"Steven, you really should stay here with us. You don't really want to be home all by yourself do you?"

"I will be ok, Aunt Patty, don't worry. I have been by myself before. I will be fine." I assured her as I walked down the hallway toward the elevator.

She followed me to the elevator and while I was waiting for the door to open she thrust a wad of money into my hand.

"You take this in case you need anything, I am going to give you my work number to call if you need me for anything. You call me, ok?" The elevator door opened and I stepped in while rolling my eyes, "You call me when you get home!" she uttered as the doors rolled shut.

I made it home a few minutes later and threw a TV Dinner into the microwave. After eating a little bit of it I decided to go next door and let John and Larissa know what had happened in case my dad hadn't called them.

None of this had surprised me. Dad had always had a very unique way of doing his mail route. Besides being drunk while he was delivering the mail, he had always refused to use a mail bag or cart for the route. Instead, he would just load up the trunk of his car every morning with the day's mail and drive to his area and grab an armful at a time while working his way from one block to the next. When he had delivered what he was carrying, he'd go back to the car to load up again. Then he would go to E.J.'s and get loaded in a different way.

When we left Jersey, dad had decided, rather than pay to bring his piece of shit car out to California, he would take the plates off of it, and just leave it parked until it got towed away. The car sat for a few months, and when it began to snow, the city had it towed. After they had towed it, they noticed that the trunk was full of undelivered mail. Mostly free samples that companies used to send to people with coupons for their products. But also some tax return checks. I am sure that my dad knew that the stuff was in there, but the fact that he left it there shows that he really didn't care.

The U.S. government did though. Once they realized who the car belonged to, the Postal Service and the FBI began investigating him for possible mail fraud. It was only a matter of time before they came and got him. After realizing that he was getting partial pension checks sent to him at his new address in San Diego, they simply waited until they knew that he would be home early one morning, and came to get him. I think that they thought that he was going through his mail and stealing things. The fact was that he was usually drunk, so he really didn't give a shit.

I really didn't think of him as a criminal. He had just made a really stupid error in judgment. After having to fend for myself for about five days, dad came home. I was let out of school early one day due to some sort of conference and when I walked through the door he was sitting on the couch smoking a cigarette.

He stood up and gave me a big hug and asked me to sit down. After explaining to me what he had done to make them arrest him, he assured me that everything would be fine. He went on for a while about what it was like for him while he was in jail. According to him, one of the worst things was that he couldn't get a decent shower. He said that the water in the shower just trickled out instead of coming out in a full stream. No mention was made of how he felt about being dragged away in front of his son, or that I had to take care of myself for a few days. He didn't have to. He knew that I was fully capable of taking care of myself if I had to. I was like a junior grown-up myself. That is how he both viewed and treated me. The amount of independence that I was granted was astonishing. I was fine with it.

Dad wound up losing his job as a result of the little vacation he took. He was having trouble finding a new one too. That was the story that he gave me. He'd get me up for school, and say that he was going to hit the streets and find a new job. I would shrug my shoulders and off I would go to class.

I later found out that he wasn't even looking for a job. One day after school, I came home to find that he was not there. This was no surprise to me. I decided to go next door and ask Larissa if she had seen him today.

"I saw him this morning laying out on the beach while I was jogging. I stopped and spoke to him for a few minutes, then I came home. He hasn't been back since. He may still be down there.", Larissa responded with a grin.

"Maybe I will go and see if he is. Thanks!", I said as I walked out the front door.

I jumped on my bike for the four-block ride to the beach and had no problem finding him laying out in his usual spot. The beach chair was on a big towel. The cooler, full of beer. There were about twenty cigarette butts sticking out of the sand next to him. Dear old dad was fast asleep with a book on his chest.

I started to turn around to head back home, but he must have sensed that I was standing there. He raised his head and looked at me with a familiar grin.

"Hey kid, what are you doing down there?", asking as he lit his smoke and grabbed a beer. "What time is it? Are you home from school already?" He had obviously been there all day and was clearly drunk. Once again, I was not the least bit surprised to find him in his present state and condition.

"Larissa said that she saw you down here, so I decided to come down and see what was going on. Is everything ok? Did you get a new job?", I asked, knowing full well that he didn't.

"I got a line on something this afternoon, and I should be starting in a day or two." Sitting up, he grabbed my hand and pulled himself out of the chair, "Help me get this stuff together, and let's get out of here."

We were walking up the hill from the beach toward the car and my bike which was chained up right next to it when he asked if I wanted to take a trip this weekend.

"If you want, we can go up to San Francisco, or maybe you want to go to Los Angeles and see some of the movie stuff."

What was I supposed to say? I knew that he wasn't doing what needed to be done to secure our lives. I knew he wasn't that concerned about finding work. What was I going to say about that? Even though he had all of this stuff going on right now, he seemed to view it as if it was just a minor thing. I really want to say something, let him know that I KNEW that he didn't have some job lined up. That was total bullshit. I don't think he knew that I was aware that he was full of it though. I was mad! I wanted to reach out and kick him the same way that I had kicked Troy and Mr. Whipple. As I pictured in my mind doing just that, I blurted out,

"Can we go and see the 'HOLLYWOOD' sign?"

"Of course, we can. We can even go up to the hill it is on and look down on it from above if you want to!!', grinning as he unlocked the hatchback for me to put my bike in the back.

That was that. We were going to go to L.A. for the weekend. Pretty soon I forgot about all of the other stuff. I was looking forward to seeing the most famous sign in the world. Everything else just seemed like a dream to me. I guess that it's pretty easy to distract the mind of a nine-year-old kid. Even one that thinks like an adult most of the time.

The trip was great! I got to go onto a real movie set, I saw the HOLLYWOOD sign. I even got the opportunity to go inside of the "Daily Planet" building that I had seen in the Superman movies, and the show Dragnet. I really believed my dad when he told me that this was really where Clark Kent worked. Later in life, I found out that it wasn't.

Before I knew it, the summer of 1985 was quickly coming. I had found that it was very easy to lose track of things like that in Southern California, due to the fact that the weather was absolutely beautiful the majority of the time.

I came home from school one afternoon to find that my key would not fit into the lock on the front door. There was a sign stuck to the front door that said Eviction Notice in big bold letters. Confused by the lock and the sign, I decided to try the back door. The same result, my key did not work, I was a pretty smart kid, but I had no idea what was going on. I didn't know what an Eviction Notice was. I also didn't know what to do next. Peering through the side windows, I could see that all of our furniture was still there. John and Larissa had moved to Arizona a few weeks prior to this, much to my personal disappointment, so I could not go next door to find out what had happened. So I decided to go down to the beach to see if my dad was around.

As usual, he was! Living our "There's No Life East of I-5" motto to its fullest. When I told him that my key did not work on the doors, he seemed a bit confused. Though I am not sure why. Obviously, he hadn't paid the rent, seeing as he didn't have a job and didn't seem to be looking for one given his current and daily state as a beach bum. I told him again that I couldn't get into the house and he just stared at me for a moment. As he rose from his slovenly position on the beach chair, his eyes showed that he realized that he and his nine-year-old child were going to be homeless.

As we drove toward the house we were now exiled from, he really didn't say much. I decided that it would be best for me to keep my mouth shut, for fear that my questions or comments might land me a hand across the mouth.

Dad tried his key in the front door and tore the sign off of it. I was sitting in the car watching with great interest. I clearly didn't understand the actual severity of the situation. Figuring that we would have to move back in with aunt Patty, I tried to relax. What I didn't know at the moment was that my dad and his sister were no longer on speaking terms. Later, I found out that after the whole FBI thing, she had loaned him a chunk of money which he had neglected to pay back. In light of his arrest, and the loans she really wanted nothing to do with him anymore.

Before he had a chance to tell me about the situation with aunt Patty, I asked him, "Dad can't we just go and stay with Aunt Patty?", he replied with a sigh,

"She said that she has washed her hands of us, she says that she has her own kids to worry about. She doesn't need two more mouths to feed.', gripping my hand tightly, "Just relax Steven, this whole thing will get worked out. We just have to wing it for a while, for now, we'll stay in the car."

Stay in the car? What the hell was that supposed to mean? I may have been young, but I wasn't stupid. There was no way that the two of us were going to be able to live out of a Toyota hatchback. My mind was filled with tons of questions as dad drove down Bayard Street. I took a last glance back at the house, thinking about my clothes and the rest of my stuff.

"What are we gonna do about our clothes?', as I stared out the window with my eyes watering up in fear. "How are we going to shower?'

Dad pulled over to the side of the road. With a quick jerk, he threw the stick into neutral, yanked the emergency brake, and turned to me,

"In a few hours, when It gets dark, we will go back to the house. You should be small enough to climb through the bathroom window.", as he looked at me with serious eyes, "You can gather up some of our things and hand them out to me, we can use the showers down at the beach to wash up for now."

Not sure what the proper response to that was supposed to be, I just said, "OK Dad, I will get our stuff. Should I still go to school tomorrow?" After looking into my eyes for a second, he told me that I should go to school while he tried to make other arrangements for us. That was that. It had been decided. My father, the guy who was always going to get it straightened out, but never did. *My Father the Idiot.*

I climbed through the window with ease as dear old dad boosted me up, holding my feet. He had told me to grab some of my clothes, a few beers out of the fridge, and the shoe box that he said was under his bed. I stumbled around in the dark with fear as I rooted through my dresser. Curious about the mysterious shoe box, I went to his room.

Crouching down, I reached under the bed and pulled out the box. I wanted to know what was in it. As I flipped the lid, I realized that my dad had more than one stash that I knew about. This thing was half full of money, and the other half stuffed with pot. I had never seen this box before today. Maybe he did know that I was pinching his stash when he wasn't around, I was already a pothead, and if he knew, he never said a word. Perhaps he didn't care.

The first night in the car was long and hot, I was curled up in the back with the seats folded down. Dad was crunched in the front seat like a sardine stuffed in a can. I didn't get much sleep, I would doze off, then I'd wake up sweating with my heart beating a million beats a minute, Worried that the police were going to find us here and drag us away. There was no way that this was legal. We were living in a car, parked by the beach, and each time I woke there was the all-too-familiar smell of pot in the air. Dad didn't seem too phased by any of this. He was in the front seat smoking a joint while I was curled up in the back, scared that this was the way I was going to spend my youth.

Daylight crept upon the car like a lion stalking its first meal in days. Rubbing the grit out of my eyes, I heard dad snoring in the front seat.

"Dad, wake up. The sun is coming up, and I'm hungry." I proclaimed as I shook his seat with the ball of my foot. With him barely stirring, I kicked the seat a little harder, "Dad!, Wake up!"

He didn't seem to want to move. After a few minutes of groaning, and me waiting impatiently for him to get up, he stretched his arms out, "What time is it?", yawning with the deliverance of a strong wind.

"I've got to get cleaned up for school, and I need to eat something." I assumed that he had forgotten that I had to go to school.

"Ok, I'm up!!" Relax will ya!" He started the car to drive down the street to one of the little bathhouses which were staggered every other block or so. This was my new bathroom. My new bedroom was rolling down the street with me in the back seat! What a life we had created in the West. Sunny California, where all of your dreams will be made a reality!! Sunny California, yeah right!!

"After school, where are you going to be?", Dad asked as we were sharing a croissant in a bistro by the beach.

"I am going to go to Jason's house for a while.", referring to my best friend at the time, "Do you want to pick me up later?", mumbling with my mouth stuffed with egg.

"Why don't you come and find me at the beach after you are done at your Jason's house? I should be down there by the time you're ready to leave.", cigarette in hand, his cup of coffee steaming away on the table like it was on fire.

Something was not right with the way he was talking to me. I could hear the defeat in his voice. I could see the quitting in his eyes. "Dad, are you alright? Are we going to be OK?" I really needed to know.

"Everything is going to be fine Son. Go to school and I will see you later.", Looking at me through slightly squinted eyes he followed up with, "It's OK, I love you! Don't worry, we'll be OK. Go on to school."

It was still early, and I knew that my friend Jason probably hadn't left for school yet, so I went to his house before heading off to school. After telling him what had happened in the past twenty-four hours, we decided to skip school and just hang out, smoke some pot, and skate on the half pipe that was in his driveway. What was the school going to do, call our parents?? Sure as shit there wouldn't be anyone there to answer my phone, and Jason's older brother would cover for him if necessary.

"Dude, I can't believe that you and your dad are living out of a car.", Jason said as he exhaled while handing me the joint to hit. "I couldn't imagine not having any place to live, that's gotta suck!"

He was a good friend, but when he said that he couldn't imagine being without a home he wasn't lying. His dad had been some sort of estate lawyer, and when he died, he left a ton of money to his two sons and wife. I had never introduced him to my dad, but he was aware of the way things had been for us in the past, so it was no surprise when he said to me,

"If you want, I can talk to my mom..." inhale, pass, exhale, "...I'm sure if we explain the situation to her, she won't have a problem with you staying here with us for a while.", Where most wealthy people would have cringed at the thought of someone like me living with them, Jason's mom was the type to take in a lost soul like myself.

"I don't know man, I am not sure that my dad will be cool with me staying here, especially if he can't stay too. I think he secretly wants me to suffer with him.", Deep down I felt like my dad sometimes saw me as a burden that he didn't need.

When I went down to the beach, later on, to hook up with dad, he was nowhere to be found. I must have walked up and down three miles of beach but to no avail. He was gone. The car was not where it usually was when he was laying out. I didn't know where he was. Maybe he had decided to leave me to fend for myself. Maybe he was in jail. Maybe he got into a car accident while driving drunk. I had no idea what to think. I had no idea what to do. I had no idea where to go.

I knocked on Jason's door with the hope that I could at least crash for the night. When his mom answered the door, I could tell from the look of concern in her eyes that she was already aware of my situation.

"Come on inside sweetie, grabbing me and giving me a quick hug, "Are you hungry? Sit down in the living room while I fix you a bite to eat.". Walking down the hallway she yelled, "JASON! Come downstairs, Steve is here!"

I felt like a moron. I knew that they just wanted to help me, but somehow I felt like I didn't do anything to deserve their help. So far my life had been a bit shaky, but I always managed to get back up when I fell. This time when I realized that dad had dropped me, I didn't feel that I was worthy of somebody else's family trying to pick me back up.

Deep down I knew that I really not only NEEDED their help. I also wanted it, but it was hard for me to let them give it to me. Just like when I refused to stay with aunt Patty, only this time I gave in and started to cry. I had to let them help me. Where else was I supposed to go? I didn't dare call my aunt. I didn't know my mother's phone number. The only chance that I had in the world was right here in a big house on Forward Street. A house that seemed like it was way too good for me, a kid from the slums of New Jersey.

I was wrong though, and after a few days of staying with the Williams family, I felt right at home. Before I knew it, almost a month had passed by. I continued to attend school. We had decided that we shouldn't make the school aware of my dad's absence. Ms. Williams said that she didn't want to see me get herded away by some state agency where I would be lost to a system that didn't really care about me. So she stood by me and became like my surrogate mother.

`We would take little day trips on weekends. They took me whale watching one Saturday and I had a blast. They even took me shopping for new clothes. It was as if I had become a real member of their family. If you didn't know any better and were introduced to Ms. Williams, you'd swear that I was one of her kids. I tried to forget everything that had happened. I wanted to try for once to live a normal life. However, I was concerned that Ms. Williams would give up her battle for my well-being eventually. But, if she was having any doubts about helping me, she wasn't showing any signs of it. To her, I was one of the kids. She never showed anything but concern and love for me.

When the principal knocked on the door and told my teacher that he needed me in the office, I wasn't sure what I should think. Why would they need me in the office? I hadn't done anything wrong that I was aware of. Could it be that they were aware of my ruse? Did something happen to my dad? Stepping down the walkway with trepidation I assumed the worst. Dad was dead. Something happened to him, He was found lifeless in a ditch somewhere. He was back in jail. The worst, that is what I expected to hear. Only what I did hear was even worse for me than I thought it would be.

He was in the principal's office waiting for me. He looked like he had lost about twenty pounds in the six weeks it had been since I had last seen him. I looked at him like he was the snake and I was the rat put into the cage with him for lunch. Standing up he outstretched his arms.

"Steven, I need to talk to you." looking over at the principal he asked, "Can you give us a minute?", "Sure", he replied, "I will be right outside." looking right at me as if he knew that I didn't want to talk to this man.

"What do you want?" I asked with an edge in my voice that I had never heard before, "I don't have anything to say to you."

"Listen, son, I am sorry, I didn't know what else to do, I had to get away. I had to be alone for a while," he stated like it was just a minor thing, leaving your child.

"You didn't know what to do!! You didn't know what to do? I can tell you what you don't do! You DON'T leave your kid with nothing and nowhere to go." screaming with every ounce of energy I had, "That's what you DON'T do!!!"

That look of defeat that I had seen that last morning at the beachside bistro was back, "Son, I am sorry, what do you want me to do? I'm...",

"I have a new family now! I don't need you anymore!! That's what I DON'T need!!", cutting him off from making more statements.

Before he could respond to my harsh words, I ran out of the office. Bumping into the principal on the way out, I yelled, "Keep that man away from me!"

I ran around the back of the school and grabbed my bike. Riding to the corner of my new street, I planned my next move. I had to see Ms. Williams. She'd know what to

43

do. I didn't think that my dad would find me there, but I wasn't sure. I decided I had to go and tell her what had happened. When I walked in the front door she seemed shocked to see me.

"Shouldn't you be in school?' she asked me, "Are you sick? What's wrong honey?"

I sat down to tell her what had happened. I half expected my dad to crash through the door at any moment while I was spilling my guts. After hearing what had happened, Ms. Williams said that she would make sure that nothing happened to me. She decided to get me away from the house for a few hours just in case my dad came looking for me.

We wound up going to the Scripps Institute, which was an Oceanographic Center a few miles away from where we were staying. I had always had a thing for the ocean. I found it to be amazing just how much was out there and was always willing to learn more about it. Ms. Williams had found out about my interest while whale watching, and used this as an opportunity to help me settle down. She called up a friend who worked at the institute and made arrangements for us to have a private tour.

We stayed for about three hours seeing everything that the place had to offer. The research labs, the dolphins, the giant models of the sea floors. I had a blast!

By the time we left Scripps, I had nearly forgotten about what had occurred earlier that morning, so you can imagine the look on my face when we pulled into the driveway to find a blue Toyota parked in it. I was terrified that I was going to be dragged away by my dad, or worse that he was going to try to do something to Ms. William. She saw the car and asked if she should call the police. I thought for a moment and told her that I would take care of it.

As we walked into the kitchen my dad was sitting at the counter with Jason. Jason looked like he had seen a ghost. He stood up, walked past me, and said,

"Dude, you need to talk to your dad. He has something important that he needs to talk to you about." with a great concern in his voice, the kind of concern only a brother or a true friend could have. To me, he was both.

I took a deep breath, grabbed Ms. Williams' hand and we walked over to the counter to sit down. "Ms. Williams, this is my dad, Dad, this is Ms. Williams."

Dad reached over to shake her hand and said "Hello," she responded with, "I am not leaving him alone, so anything you have to say, you are going to have to say in front of me."

Saying that he understood, he went on to tell me that my grandmother, his mother, was in the hospital and that we had to go back to New Jersey as soon as possible. He was here both to apologize, and to collect me so that we could return back East to take care of her. I didn't want to hear it. I didn't want to leave California, I wanted to stay here with The Williams. By my posture, and my eye-rolling, all of that was clear. Ms. Williams caught on to it quickly and asked me to give her a minute alone to talk to my dad.

I went upstairs to Jason's room and we spoke for a few minutes about what my dad had said. Dad had explained the situation to him. I didn't know what to feel. Sure I loved my Nanny, as we referred to my grandmother, but I wasn't sure that returning back East to take care of her was what I wanted. It wasn't my responsibility, was it? Maybe it was dad's but not mine. Since he had decided that I was no longer his responsibility when he left me homeless, I made the distinction that his affairs were no longer my own.

I decided to go back downstairs to see what was going on with my dad and Ms. Williams. They were in the kitchen having coffee and talking when I walked in. Motioning me over to sit down, my new caretaker said to me,

"Steven, your father and I have been talking and I really think you need to understand what is going on here. Your grandmother really needs someone right now to take care of her, and your father has to go and do it."

I looked at him with disdainful eyes. Wanting to tell him that he was ruining my life and said, "Why can't you go alone? I'll stay out here until she is better and then you can come back."

Dad hadn't said a word by that point, and when he decided to answer my question, he had tears in his eyes, "As soon as Nanny is better, we will come back. I know that you don't want to be in New Jersey. Neither do I!", repeating himself, "As soon as I can get her settled, we will pack up and come back." He opened his arms to me, and I felt that I needed to hug him.

"Do you promise that we will come back Dad?", hugging him with tearful eyes, "Of course we will, I promise."

That was the end of it. We were leaving in the morning for the three-thousand-mile drive back to New Jersey. After discussing it, Ms. Williams told dad that he could sleep on the couch while I slept upstairs. She wanted us both to get a good night's rest for our long trip.

She woke up early the next morning. It wasn't even daylight out yet. She made sure that we both ate a hearty breakfast. She helped us get our things together for the trip. She even stocked a big cooler full of lunchmeat, snacks, and soda for us to eat on the road. It was hard for me to say goodbye to Jason. He had become just like my brother. I thought I would never see him again. If it was hard for me to part with him, then it was nearly impossible for me to leave his mom. This woman was like no one I had ever met before. She cared for me like I was her own. To me, that was the greatest thing in the world.

As I hugged her, she whispered in my ear, "Don't worry kiddo, I will see you when you get back, you will always be welcome here!!!"

SAN DIEGO -TO- NJ
JUNE 1985

I didn't know it at the time, but that would be the last time I would ever see Jason or Ms. Williams again. There was never any real intention by my dad to ever return to California to live.

Dad had planned the trip for us to make it back to my Nanny's house in just over three days. We were to cut along the southwest until we were through the Texas panhandle, then head north through Oklahoma, and Missouri, until we were finally traveling Northeast from Illinois on through to toward our final destination; The Grungy State of New Jersey.

The first day was uneventful. Just long and empty stretches of barren desert in Arizona and New Mexico. After spending the night in a Motel 6 outside of Albuquerque, we began the second day going through Texas and Oklahoma before stopping for the night in Joplin, Missouri, The panhandle of Texas really smelled like cow shit! Never in my life had I had such a scent suck in my nostrils before.

Dad didn't really say a whole lot about our current situation while we were driving, He never uttered a single word about what he was doing during his six-week sabbatical from parenting. I wondered a few times what was going on in that head of his as he was driving along humming with the songs on the radio. While we were having a lunch outside of Indianapolis, I said to my dad,

"Dad, wouldn't it be great if Nanny was already out of the hospital by the time we got back?" In my head that would make my hopeful return West even sooner. "That would be wonderful son." he retorted while stuffing a burger into his mouth, "Hopefully she will be!!"

I was hoping for the best! After three and a half days on the road we were heading into my hometown of Hillside, New Jersey, My Nanny lived just five blocks from the house I had lived in when I was with my mother. My mother had since then remarried and was living down by the shore with her new husband, my new stepfather David, my sister Nicole and my brother Robert. My mother's parents still lived in the apartment downstairs from the one that she was living in when I left. I was looking forward to seeing my other grandparents, as well as my mom.

As we walked up the stairs to Nanny's apartment, she opened the door and rushed out to give us both a hug. Oddly she didn't look like she had been in the hospital. She did look old, but she didn't look sick. Certainly not sick like my dad claimed she was when we departed East. I started to wonder if she was sick at all. Was all of this just a ploy to get me to come back to Jersey without incident??"

HILLSIDE -&- HOWELL, NJ
SUMMER 1985

A few days after we got settled in at Nanny's house, I spoke to my mom for the first time in almost two years. She told me that she had just moved into a new house that was built just for her, so she was trying to get settled in too. After discussing it with my dad, she told me that wanted me to come down to her new house in a few weeks to spend the rest of the summer. Easily distracted from the now obvious sleight of hand trick that dad had just pulled, I agreed to go. I was actually excited about seeing the rest of my family. Dad and Nanny took me out and bought me a new bike to take with me since I had left my old one in San Diego.

About two and a half weeks later, Nanny drove me to my mother's new home. Dad had just started a new job so he wasn't able to make the trip down.

I was so boisterous talking about my great life that I was living out in California. Taking every chance boasting to any and everyone who would listen. I didn't say anything about the problems that we had encountered out there. My dad had discussed it with me, and we decided that no one needed to know about what we had been through, "It's nobody's business but ours Steven." were the words he used. He also thought it best that I didn't tell my mother that I was going to be moving back west. "She just wouldn't take it well if she knew you were moving away again. Trust me."

Not knowing any better, I took my dad's word that I shouldn't run my mouth about those things. That didn't stop me from explaining all of the other stuff that I had seen between Jersey and California and back again.

I stayed down the shore until the middle of August. Spending my days running around the neighborhood with Nicole ,Robert and my stepsister Evie. Going swimming in mom's swimming pool daily, as well as at the beach. I had enjoyed myself immensely all summer long, and before I knew it, it was time to go back to school again. Back to Hurden Looker Elementary.

Hurden Looker was the same school I had attended from kindergarten through second grade. The same school that I went to when my parents split. So it was no surprise to me that I had to have a meeting with the principal and the school counselor before I was allowed to return. After all, some of these teachers are the same ones that I was throwing desks and chairs at just three years before.

As I strolled through the hallways of the fifth grade, I was aware of the looks that I got from some of the faculty there. They all knew who I was and what I had done at that school before and I suspected that they were aware of the problems that I encountered at my last school. They were watching me, I was watching them. Hell, I was watching them watch me. I thought it best to try to behave and see how this whole thing played out.

I got through the first half of the year without incident, and during Christmas break, I spent a few days at mom's house. Nicole and Robert came to stay with my other grandparents a few blocks away so they could spend some time with our dad.

The snow was falling and I was almost a normal kid again. I still missed the West but was confident that I would get my chance to return. Meanwhile, I would run around Hillside with my friends, throwing snowballs at passing cars and just plain doing what kids my age did.

School started back up again after New Year's, and even though I dreaded going back, I needed something to do. Just running around the neighborhood in the winter was not doing it for me. I wanted the warm weather back!! If I couldn't get it from the West coast, then all I could do was look forward to the coming Spring and Summer.

It was the end of April when dad came home and told me about his new girlfriend down the shore. I wasn't surprised that he had found a new woman at all. Over the past few years, he had plenty of them. This one, he said was different, "I really like this one!! She can't wait to meet you!!", Like a love-stricken teen. He told me that we were going to be moving out of Nanny's house and moving in with Nikki the day after school let out for the year. I didn't take the news well, but merely replied, "Sure Dad, fine!!"

NEPTUNE, NJ
JUNE 1986

Jumping Brook Apartment Complex looked like a strip of cheap Monopoly houses glued together end by end and dropped on a patch of land half a mile off of the Garden State Parkway and Route 33. It was the kind of place that you would see in a movie where every kid in the neighborhood had some sort of weird cancer and the people couldn't explain what was going on, but they knew something was not right. That is how I saw it. So when I recognized that this was going to be my new home I just cringed with a new type of disgust. When I met Nikki, that disgust changed into a deep hatred for both her and her shitty apartment.

I knew right away from the moment that I first met her that not only was she wrong for my dad, but she was wrong for me. Nikki owned a little beauty parlor about a block's distance away from this strip of crap. When I first saw the velvet wallpaper in her apartment, and the matching print on the couch, the only thing that I could think of was the prizes that people could buy when they spent their winnings at the end of Wheel of Fortune, "I'll take the Velvet Elvis and the matching loveseat Pat!" Immediately that was my vision of this woman's lack of taste. She looked down at me when I first met her and grinned an obviously fake grin,

"What a pleasure to meet you, young man, Your father has told me so much about you!!", like a witch looking into her cauldron with feasting eyes on the assortment of little children that she was going to boil into a stew. Yeah, right lady, I thought, you want me around just as much as I want you around.

Rather than say what I was thinking, I just smiled and said in a perfect tone, "It's really nice to finally meet you, Nikki, what a great place."

The look in her eye was clear. She knew that I could see right through her, I knew that she was aware of my discovery. But I thought, what can you do bitch?? Hmm? You may be his girlfriend right now, but I will always be his son. You ain't always gonna be his girlfriend. Looking at her my eyes glinted as if to say, you have no chance. Her's reflected back, Try me!!

The first night we went out for dinner and made small talk about the usual things. Dad seemed happy that Nikki and I were getting along, but that was just a show for his sake. We knew differently, I was sitting there listening to her cackle on about this and that, while the whole time trying to figure out how I was going to break up their relationship. I couldn't tell dad how I felt, he would just tell, "Give it a chance, she's great, you'll see.", but I would see. I plotted on her and she sat across the table with the same thing in mind. How can I get rid of the kid???

Dad was oblivious to our little visual challenge. He seemed like he was enjoying the fact that we seemed to be hitting it off. Maybe he was just trying to find me the stability that he knew I needed. Trying to make up for the lack of real parenting that he had been providing thus far.

Although I could respect his efforts to find me a new female role model, there was no way that I was going to let this woman be it. Nikki was just so wrong for both of us. As much as I wanted to have a female figure around, I couldn't accept this witch.

    Since those days when I was a child, I've often commented on dad's relationship with Nikki by claiming that I was so used to it being just the two of us. So when this other woman came into the picture, I felt like she was trying to take my dad away from me. Looking back now, I realize that there was more to it than that. She actually didn't want me around, as I later found out. But there was something else, I was willing to share my father's attention with someone else. I had done it before, back in Bayonne, he had been dating a woman named Phylis for a few years. She was great. Phylis had three kids, each of them older than me by increments of 2 years. When they were dating, we often spent every weekend at her house. Sometimes we wouldn't return to our own place for more than a week or two. I think that the biggest difference between the relationship with Nikki compared to Phylis was the children, Phylis had kids, but Nikki didn't. Phylis' ability to have a motherly presence came to her naturally. Nikki saw me as some sort of adversary, To her, I was the one trying to steal my dad away. Trying to keep cupid from shooting his arrow. I was the problem, In reality, that was true, But not for the reason she thought. I just knew that she was not capable of being a mother to me. Regardless of the way that she felt about my father, I knew that she was wrong, and I was about to prove it.

    Since Nikki owned the beauty parlor, she was gone all day most of the time, Dad was working at a new job, so he wasn't around either. I went back to my role as an unsupervised child. I used my time alone in the house to try to find some sort of dirt to us against their growing relationship. I would spend all day long going through everything she owned to try to find something that I could present to dad to make him realize that she wasn't right for us. As I searched, I found a lot of things, but much to my dismay, nothing seemed applicable, There was her stash of porno movies and sex toys, but dad was a liberal-minded guy. He used to share his own porn with me, Even at such a young age, His rationale was that there was absolutely nothing wrong with the human body, often commenting,

"The human body is a beautiful thing, Steven. If you want to look at naked magazines, that is fine. Just keep in mind that these women are creatures to be worshiped, not abused." He always had a way of making me see things in a different light. But he was right. It is perfectly normal for a young growing boy to want to see a naked woman. Sex had always been an open issue with my dad. Often I would hear him and his girlfriends going at it in the next room late at night.

Even the sex toys that Nikki had didn't seem like something that I could use to paint her as a deviant. I may not have known exactly what a dildo was back then, but I knew what it looked like. I also had a pretty good idea what she did with it. So I realized that dad would probably enjoy watching her use it.

As you may have guessed, drugs weren't an issue for us either. Dad smoked, and I smoked. So when I discovered Nikki's assortment of substances, I knew that I couldn't use that as ammunition either. Being the person that I was, I thought, I had no problem using them to enlighten my thought process. I would grab a little bit of pot every day, smoking it while I searched the house.

It was in the midst of one of my altered state search parties that I found something that even if I couldn't use to get rid of her, I could use to make myself feel like I wasn't wasting my time, In her closet, I came across one of those small fire-proof lock boxes which was full of cash. This was more cash than I had ever seen. Full of twenty, fifty, and hundred dollar bills. I was astounded by my new discovery. As greed and temptation set in, I figured that if I couldn't get rid of her, then at least I could spend the fruits of her labor. I started out by just taking a few of each denomination. About four hundred sixty dollars. Not exactly sure how I was going to spend the money, I decided to call a cab to take me to the Seaview Square Mall, which was about fifteen minutes away.

I roamed around for a few hours buying a small assortment of G.I. Joe and Transformer action figures to add to my collection back home. I didn't want to get a lot of stuff right away. I wanted to buy things that would blend in with the toys that I already had. I figured that I could boost my toy stock little by little so that no one would catch on to my deed.

This went on for about two weeks. Dad and Nikki would leave for work, and I would go shopping. Sometimes it was the Seaview Square Mall, and others it was the Monmouth Mall, Which was a little further away. I would bring home bags of goodies. Stashing them in the basement of the apartment complex. I didn't want to keep my newly gotten treasures in the house for fear of getting caught.

One day, after hanging around in the back of the building playing with my toys, I met a few of the local kids. They were all impressed with my assortment of new toys. These were the toys that most kids had to wait until Christmas or their Birthday to get. But I had already gotten mine. They were instantly latched onto me, I don't have a problem sharing my stuff. I would often give brand-new toys away to some of the other kids. So it was no surprise to me when some of the older kids came around looking for a handout.

As I was standing by the local ice cream truck buying cones for everyone who was around, I was approached by a kid named Dave who was about three years older than I was.

"Hey little dude, are ya gonna buy me a cone too?", He asked with a devious grin, "Everyone else got one for free, so what about me??" Half expecting me to be intimidated by him. What did I care? It wasn't my money that I was spending, it was Nikki's. I wasn't scared of this kid, I just didn't give a crap about blowing the money. After all, there was more where that came from. You can imagine his surprise when I handed him a fifty-dollar bill and told him,

"Here man buy whatever you want. I've got plenty!" like it was no big deal at all. It really wasn't. He just stood there for a second dumbfounded before he grabbed the money that I was holding out., "See ya later dude," I replied as I was walking away.

After about twenty seconds, I could hear him chasing me down yelling, "Hey...kid...wait up will ya!" deep breaths between words. "Where are you running off to? Let's hang out and go and do something. " I stopped, and when he caught his breath, I looked at him cautiously, replying,

"OK, what do you want to do?", half expecting him to try and rob me for my money, "Wanna go and smoke a joint?" I asked in order to distract his possible intentions.

"Damn kid, how old are you!?, he yelped as he was laughing at the boldness of my inquiry, "Yeah man, let's go and smoke a joint.", chuckling as we walked down the street, "You got one?"

"Come with me.", walking him towards my building. I figured that it would be kind of cool to hang out with someone older than me, especially someone who could look up at me because of my newfound wealth, instead of looking down at me like I was just some little shit.

We smoked a joint and laughed a lot as I told him about the crazy bitch that my dad was dating. A little while later after I told him that my dad would be home soon. Say that we could screw around down there for a while.

"My buddies are down at my place right now, so let's go over there. My mom is working late. We can order some pizza and maybe rent some videos", offering options as we were walking down the street toward his place. I called my dad a little while later and asked if it was ok if I hung out with my new friend for a few more hours. Telling me that it was ok, he also offered,

"You can spend the night if you want, just make sure you call me in the morning so I know you're alright."

It went on like this for a week or so. I would spend my days hanging out with Dave and the rest of my new and older friends. We would go to the mall and hang out.

We would skateboard around the parking lots in the area. We even went shopping for high-speed remote control cars to race at the little track down the road. Of course, I paid for all of our cars, but I didn't mind. They didn't seem to mind either. Dave knew where I was getting my money from and he had told me that I should do something to stick it to the bitch that my dad was banging. I couldn't agree more, I had once again escaped the dark side of my ever-present bad surroundings. Just like living with the Williams' was blinding my reality from my eyes, spending Nikki's money was making me forget that I hated her with every bit of my soul.

One day, after I skated back from Dave's house, I found my dad with Nikki waiting in the living room for me to get home. Dad didn't even give me the chance to say anything, he just reached out and smacked me harder than he ever had before. He hit me again, and again, and again until I couldn't tell where his hand ended and my face began. I was screaming out, my eyes filled with tears, my breathing in little gasps,

"Dad, stop, what are you doing, I didn't do anything, Stop!", repeating myself over and over, "Stop, I didn't do anything!"

Dizzy from the hits, I stumbled to the ground and just lay there crying, Why was my dad beating me? I only wanted him to leave her, I didn't do it to try to make him mad.

"You think that you can steal from us?", shouting as I lay on the ground like a lumpy pile of flesh. Us? What did he just say? Us? I wasn't taking anything from him, It was from her.

"I hate her dad, I HATE HER!" looking over at Nikki, "I hate you!! I don't want you to be with my dad", with a glare that could cut through steel, "He's too good for you!!"

Dad would have no part in this, he grabbed me and started to drag me toward the couch, "I want to go and live with mommy, I hate it here.", as I was being thrown down.

"You want to go and live with your mother? That is exactly what you are going to get. Let her deal with your shit. I don't need it anymore!", while ranting as he was grabbing my belongings up and stuffing them into a big black trash bag. "You are going to your mother's", slamming one of my new toys against the wall. Still repeating the same phrase over and over, "..Your mother's".

Nikki just stood there with her arms crossed and finally replied,

"Little bastard should be put in jail. That would serve him right!!", before coming over and smacking me across the face really hard.

She hit me! That crusty bitch hit me. I was suddenly irate. Charging at her the way a bull charges at a rodeo clown, I began to hit and kick her with all of my energy. Then all of a sudden I couldn't see anything, It was black.

To this day I am still not sure just where dad had struck me, or with what. One thing is for sure, I was unconscious. The next thing I knew, I was waking up in the back seat of the car. We were heading down the Garden

State Parkway toward my mother's house, I didn't say a word. Neither did my dad. He just drove.

When we approached her house, he pulled into the driveway. Opening the passenger door, he only uttered two words, "Get Out!", I complied, and he proceeded to take all of my belongings out of the hatch.

Once my things were in a neat pile near the garage door, he silently got back in the car without even acknowledging me, backed out of the short driveway, and drove off down the street. I wasn't sure what to think. I expected mom to come outside and greet me. She didn't. I walked up the stairs to the front door, pressed the doorbell, and waited for a moment. Nothing. No answer. Clearly, there was nobody home.

I grabbed my stuff and started to cart it around the back of the house to wait on the patio until someone came home. Plugging my thirteen-inch black and white TV into the outlet on the back of the house, I settled into a lounge chair to wait. Hours went by without anyone. My head throbbed from the beating I had taken. I was hungry. There was nothing that I could do but wait.

After what seemed like an eternity, I heard a car pull into the driveway and the garage door open. I jumped up and ran around to the front of the house to embrace my mother. She looked at me with the confusion of a dog whimpering at its master. She was not expecting me. That much was very clear. She just stared at me for a second before asking,

"Steven, what are you doing here?? How long have you been out here waiting? What happened to your face?", the side of her hand lightly brushing my cheek.

"Dad dropped me off, Mommy. He said that I can't live with him anymore. His girlfriend doesn't want me around...Can I live here with you?", I questioned while trying to hug her.

"What? What do you mean dropped you off? Where did he go?". Full of questions that I didn't really have the answer to. "Come inside.", taking my hand to lead me into the house. Nicole and Robert seemed happy to see me, although the look on their faces also showed a hint of confusion.

Once inside, I explained everything to my mother. I told her about Nikki, our moving to Neptune, and the money. I further explained the ass whipping that I took as a result of my behavior. Telling her that dad let Nikki hit me as well.

"He even let her hit me..." while sobbing, "Then he knocked me out...Please don't make me go back there Mom!"

She didn't seem to know how to respond. Sitting there with a blank look on her face, she showed no real emotion. I am sure that she was concerned for me, but her face read like an empty page.

"I don't know what to do Steven. I need to speak with your father about this. I don't think David is going to allow you to live here full time.", referring to my new stepfather, with whom I really didn't get along very well.

To my mother, letting me stay for a weekend at a time, or a few weeks during the summer was one thing. But opening her happy home to me indefinitely was something that she could not even begin to imagine. The main problem was David. He and I had numerous problems since I had met him. I would never be willing to see him as an authority figure. So when he tried to tell me what to do, I just plain didn't do it. In my eyes, it was my father who had the authority to try and discipline me, not him. In David's eyes, it was his job to do the disciplining in their home. Mom wasn't much of an authority figure. She would leave that to the new man of the house. So it became clear to me that there was no way that this man was going to allow me to live in his home.

Unfortunately, mom was unable to stand up to David when it came to me. If he didn't want me there, then that was the bottom line. She was not willing to fight for the life of her son. Maybe it was because of the hell that I put her through five years prior to this, or maybe she didn't want to take the chance on me ruining the happy life that she'd developed since my dad split. Either way, I was out.

I begged and pleaded, I promised to behave. "Mom, I will be good, don't make me go back there with him." Hoping that she would give in., "I don't want to be around that woman, I hate her." mom just dialed the phone and told my father to come and get 'His' son. That was that. There was nothing that I could do. I would have to go back to Neptune and face the music. Dad would have to deal with me instead of just pawning me off on my mother.

After picking me up, he drove home in complete silence. I tried to fight the urge to scream. I didn't want to see that skank Nikki again. I had such a deep disgust for her. I just wanted it to be me and my dad again. Two guys out on the road of life. No life East of I-5!! I wanted that back. Dad had other plans.

As we walked in the door, he pointed to my bedroom, "You are not to come out of that room for any reason whatsoever! Do you understand me?",

"What about my stuff? Aren't you going to bring my stuff inside?", as I trembled. "What if I have to use the bathroom?"

Dad slammed the door shut, "Hold it in!!", he retorted.

Sitting in my bedroom, I couldn't even begin to imagine the punishment that I would be subjected to now that I was back in my dad's house. Surely I would be grounded for a long time. I would have to find a way to pay back Nikki. Who knew what else he would put me through to defend the honor of his new lady. I wasn't even allowed to use the bathroom for crying out loud. What else would he do? He could beat me again. He could make me apologize. He could even try to make Nikki and I try to get along. Like all of the other drama that we had been through over the years, I figured that this would eventually go away. But first I would have to take the punishment that he lai out.

One thing was for sure, the punishment that I was expecting paled in comparison to the punishment that I actually received for my actions. In a million years, there was no way that I could imagine what would be in store for me the following morning.

THE MORNING THAT CHANGED EVERYTHING
JUNE 1986

I was awakened suddenly by my dad grunting, "Get the fuck up and put on your clothes. You've got two minutes." Judging from the amount of sun coming through the window, it was still early in the morning. Grabbing my clothes, I wasn't sure what to think. Maybe he was getting me up to make me perform some menial labor task to work off the money that I had taken? Once I was dressed, I went out to the living room and dad said,

"C'mon lets go." grabbing his keys and escorting me through the front door. "I don't want to hear one fucking word out of you, got it?"

Where are we going?" I so desperately wanted to ask him, but I was scared that he would turn around and smack the hell out of me. Instead, I just trudged along the walkway to the car and got in without a word. Dad walked to the car and got in silently. He still hadn't taken my stuff out of the car, so when I got in, I started to reach into the backseat to grab a comic book.

"Leave that shit alone, Just sit there and be still and quiet.", without even looking at me. He started the car and headed down the road. Ten minutes later we were there.

He pulled around the side of the hospital toward a nondescript building just off the side of the main parking lot. I saw a small sign on the door which read *'Family Services'* and just started quizzically. The car stopped, and I was tempted to ask dad what we were doing here. I decided to just go along with it.

"Come on!", he grunted as he pushed me up the stairs. Once inside, he approached the desk and said to the old and weathered, blond receptionist,

"We have an eight-thirty appointment to speak with Caseworker Andrews.",

She nodded at him while glancing over at me with apologetic eyes "It's just down the hall, second door on the right."

I followed him into the room and was told to sit down once again. A woman came out of the adjacent office and approached my father. "Robert? I'm Carol Andrews", pointing toward her office, "Come on in and have a seat." He looked at me, "Stay Put!", he said with vengeful eyes.

I sat down and waited for him to come back out. About ten minutes later, a man with a gray beard and clothes that seemed to come from a thrift store came out and approached me.

"Steve? I am John Anderson, I would like to talk to you for a while if that is ok with you."

Not sure what I should say, I stood up and said, "Uh, ok, sure" and followed him down the hallway to yet another office. He pointed to a seat and I sat down as he closed the door.

"I am a Case Manager for the Division of Youth and Family Services. Do you know what that is?", asking me as he sat down behind his enormous desk.

"Um, No!" I responded while looking around the wood-paneled room full of important-looking plaques stuck to the wall in no obvious pattern. "What's youth and..."

Cutting me off, he answered, "The Division of Youth and Family Services, DYFS for short is an agency that helps children out in certain situations, Like the one you have with your dad and his girlfriend..um..", pausing to look down at a notepad,

"Nikki", I interjected, "Her name is Nikki, and I hate her.". With the crassness of a spoiled brat.

"Yes, Nikki..well, anyhow, as I was saying, we are here to help out in special situations that families may go through. You say you hate her, tell me more about that. Why is that.", repeating himself one more time, "Why do you hate her?"

"She's not for him. I know that she is totally wrong for my dad. She doesn't like me either, She just wants to pull us apart.", I blurted out, starting to get myself worked up just thinking about her.

"Go on, tell me more.", scribbling with a pen to write something down, "Does she make you angry when you see her?"

"Can we talk about something else? I don't want to talk about her.", wondering again why I was really here.

"Sure young man, what would you like to talk about?", he asked, staring down from his seat at me like I was supposed to know the answer.

"I don't know.", he cut in with, "Tell me a little about your life. What do you like to do? Do you like sports? Do you have any hobbies?"

What was this, an interview for summer camp? What did my hobbies have to do with anything? Who was this guy? Why was he asking me all of these questions?

"Why am I here?", I asked him, shifting in my seat to try to get comfortable.

"Steven, I am only here to help you get through this. I want you to think of me as a friend. You can tell me anything that you would like, and it will go no further than this room.", he answered with great concern in his voice.

I could smell the stale odor of pipe tobacco in the air. "Help me get through what?", I asked him.

"Listen, son, your father has told us about what occurred the other day. He asked us to try and help you with some of your problems, he only wants what's best for you."

I could not understand what was happening. It was as if I was suddenly out of breath and this guy was going to make me pay for the next one, "Where is my dad?"

"Your father has left. We are going to be taking care of you from now on.", pausing to adjust something on the desk, "We are going to put you in a new home with a new family."

"What do you mean my dad left? Where did he go? I don't want to stay here anymore.", I jumped up, and ran for the door to escape. The knob wouldn't turn. I was trapped.

"Son, calm down.", he grabbed me. Oddly he didn't grab me in a harsh way, more like the way you would embrace someone who had just lost a loved one. "You are going to be ok, Just try and calm down. We will help you."

I was defeated. There was nowhere to run. I was at the mercy of this place, whatever it was. I sat back down and he asked if I wanted something to drink, "Maybe a soda?, or whatever you like.", I nodded and he pushed a button on the telephone. When it beeped back, he spoke into it, "Marci, Can you bring in a..hold on." looking at me, "What kind of soda son?", "Root Beer!" I answered. Speaking back into the phone, "Root Beer, and a snack.", looking again at me, "Are you hungry?", I nodded yes,

Once I calmed down, He explained to me that I was going to have to go and stay with a new family because my dad felt that he could no longer take care of me. I would be going to meet them in a little while, He asked me if I understood.

I nodded, "I think so. I'm going to get a new home to live in. Right?", trying to process the whole thing in my head. I didn't understand. I had heard what he said, and although I knew what it meant, I didn't understand why it was happening to me. I may not have been the best-behaved kid on the planet, but did I deserve to be carted away like some orphan in a movie? I only wanted things to be the way they were. Just me and my dad. Just the two of us against the world. Now I saw that it was every man for himself. Dad had made that decision when he decided to disown me.

I shouldn't have been surprised. He had left me once before. Why wouldn't he do it again? I would have been better off if he had just left California without me. He could have left me with the Williams family. At least there I could have been provided with a loving home with people that I was comfortable with. Now I was at the mercy of some agency that doled out orphaned kids.

That was it. I was alone. My life would never be the same after that. I was on the wrong side of a society that had taken everything that I cared about away from me. While offering me nothing in return. These were the same sort of people that Ms. Williams said would drag me away if they had found out that dad had disappeared that day in San Diego. I took a deep breath. Hoping that there would be some sort of silver lining to this dark cloud that was thrown over my head. There had to be something good in all of this. There just had to be. With all that I had been through thus far, I could only hope that this would turn out okay for me. I imagined that my mom would come and rescue me, or that my dad would come bursting through the door at any second to say that he had changed his mind. Maybe he would want me back. Maybe Ms. Williams would find out what had happened to me and come to New Jersey to adopt me. I could only hope for the best.

A second case worker came into the office and sat down next to me. Putting her hand on mine, she said to me,

"Steven, I know that this is hard for you, but I assure you that we will help you get through this.", with the attentiveness of a concierge, "Whatever you need, we will take care of it. Trust me, you will be fine."

She went on to explain some more about the foster care program. I was to be placed with a family from Middletown, named the Pinkam's. They had three other children, none of them fosters. They were looking forward to meeting me. She rambled on about little details that didn't matter to me one bit. I didn't need a dossier on these people. I needed a way out of this. I needed salvation from the arms of the life that had embraced me in its cold and dark grip. No matter what this woman or anyone else told me, I know that it wasn't going to be ok. I knew that this was the end of the life that I had known. I recognized the beginning of something that would weigh me down for a long time to come. I'm not sure how I knew it, but I did.

Deep inside of my skull I could feel this pressure. I would come to know this feeling very well through the years. My life had become like a giant migraine. A crushing pain between my ears that no amount of medication could fix.

THE PINKAM RESIDENCE: MIDDLETOWN, NJ JUNE 1986

As the car approached the long and steep driveway, I was overcome by a sudden fear. As much as I wanted to be accepted and loved by someone,....anyone, I was scared that I would be abandoned again, and again until there was nothing left for me. The only solution to this that I could think of was not to give anyone the chance to get close to me. If they didn't grow to like me, then I wouldn't have to worry about them loving or leaving me. I would just make them hate me. I would try to be as crass as I could. Then they wouldn't want to give me a chance. Maybe if I behaved badly enough, this DYFS place would have to give up on me and drop me back off with dad. The same way that he dropped me off with them. That was my solution. I would show them!

I was led through the front door to find my new pseudo-family waiting for me with toothy grins. Shifting my weight slightly to one side, I looked at them, waiting for someone to speak. Finally the woman stretched her hand out and spoke,

"You must be Steve. I am JoAnne Pinkam.", pointing to herself. Yeah obviously lady, I thought. I got the 'I am' part when you said your name, no need to point.

"This is my husband Jim", again pointing, "And this is Cheryl, Scott, and over there in the walker", pointing once again, "is little Andrew. It's so nice to meet you."

"Uh, yeah, nice to meet you too", rolling my eyes at the whole bunch. Surveying the living room, I spied a total of twelve crucifixes, and four Mary statues. The plaid couch had a crocheted afgan draped over it, and there was a sign above the doorway which said 'Jesus Saves'. Where the hell was I? I expected the guy from Candid Camera to come through the door at any minute dressed like The Pope. In the air was the smell of Murphy's Oil Soap. I recognized the smell from somewhere, but couldn't place it. Then it hit me. That is what my Grandmother's church smelled like. How fitting, I thought.

"Would you like to see your room son?", the gangly father said to me with a trucker's tone. "Come on, I will show you around.", as the rest of the bunch just stood there with their big ivory grins, like a bunch of robots waiting for their next command.

"Over here is the kitchen.", pointing to the left as we walked through the dining room. "Down there is our bedroom, and the bathroom.", pointing further beyond the kitchen, "Cheryl's room is also down there.", he aptly stated as we continued going down the hallway into a rec room. "And right over there is your room.", pointing to a doorway on the far side of the room, which had an assortment of children's toys scattered about. "Scott's room is next to yours. You guys have the whole right side of the house.", waving his arms around the room. "Well then, let's get you settled in before supper, shall we?"

I looked around the room for a minute. Where is the TV?, I wondered. There wasn't one in the living room. There wasn't one here in the rec room. It had to be around here somewhere. I'd find it later. I followed him back out into the living room where the rest of the congregation was still waiting. Still in the same position as we had left them.

Heading toward the door, he said, "Scott, come and help us get this young man's things.", "Sure Daddy!", the kid answered in his best fashion. We unloaded the car and carried my things into the living room where they were placed in neat little piles.

"Don't you want to take these into my room?" I asked when we were finished. The man looked at me and said, "Not right now. I want to check through your stuff first and make sure that you don't have anything that you shouldn't have. We run a tight ship around here." he stated, "We wouldn't want you to go and have something that could harm one of us, now would we?"

What did he think I was? Some sort of ax murderer? I was the victim in this situation. It wasn't the other way around. What did he think that I could have in my things that would warrant him searching them? I shrugged it off and followed him into the kitchen. The lady was feeding some sort of brownish dough into a device that seemed to be turning it into spaghetti noodles. "What is that!?", I shouted in a confused tone.

"I am making whole wheat spaghetti for dinner.", she said as she looked up from her task. My nostrils flared from the odor of this creation. I had never heard of whole wheat spaghetti before.

"Why are the noodles whole wheat?", I inquired. "What's wrong with regular noodles?", it didn't make sense to me. The average person would just open a box of spaghetti and throw it into a pot of boiling water. "What do they taste like?", I asked, not really wanting to hear the answer.

"In this house, we only eat what is good for us. We only do what's good for us.", standing over the stove in a stoutly manner, "God provides us with many blessings. Our body is our temple, the least we can do is take care of it"

God? Blessings? Whole Wheat Spaghetti? Temples? What the hell was this woman talking about? My grandmother was a church going woman. She was also one hundred percent Italian. I never saw her making whole wheat noodles, or heard her talk about damn temples. This lady had to be nuts.

A while later, as we sat down to eat, Mr. Pinkam looked at me from across the table and said, "In light of the fact that the Lord has blessed us with a new addition to our home, I think that our new guest should lead us in the saying of Grace, Steven, Go ahead."

What? I didn't know what to say. I had never said Grace before, I didn't know any prayers. Looking at them with their heads bowed, I was at a loss for words. I had nothing. He looked up and glanced at me. "I don't know what that is.", I stated plainly.

"Son, If you are going to eat at our table, and eat the food that the Lord has provided for you, then you are going to learn how to say Grace.", sighing at my lack of theological procedure, "I will do it.", he grunted.

We bowed our heads, and he ranted off some prayer that didn't sound familiar to me. When he was finished, he looked up and said to his wife, "What are you thankful for?"
"I am thankful for all of our blessings, and I am thankful that the Lord has sent us a new child to help.", she peered over in my direction and smiled, "I am also

thankful that we have been provided with the bounty to be able to feed our family."

What the hell was she talking about? As I started to wonder what was wrong with these kooks, Mr. Pinkam looked over at the kids and asked them the same question. They rambled on about various odds and ends, the food, Me, the food and so on. Beginning to get frustrated, I put my head in my hands and gripped the top of my hair very tight. I knew it was coming. I knew it!

"Steven, what are you thankful for Son?", he asked.

What was with all of this 'Son' shit? I thought. Looking at him with a face that might scare the Devil himself,

"I AM NOT THANKFUL FOR ANYTHING! CAN WE EAT NOW?",I snapped at him.

I could see from the look in his eyes that he wanted to get up from the table and choke the life out of me. There was a dark secret in those eyes of his that I could easily see. Regardless of the whole religious thing, I knew that he had his own demons. I wanted to release them. I wanted to bring out of him what he so desperately wanted to keep hidden.

Instead of getting up, he just took a deep breath and softened the look on his face and said, "Well, it's obvious that this young man has had a rough day, so maybe it's best if we just eat dinner.", reaching for the pasta, he looked over at me and said, "Would you like some spaghetti?" I nodded and took the plate from him. Out of nowhere, I followed up with, "Thank you.", I am not sure where it came from, but I said it. Here I was, trying to set this man off on me, and he didn't take the bait. He just let it brush right by him. I was still angry. Why did I thank him? I was raised with manners, even if I didn't always exercise them. I guess the good side of me came into the light. If only for a moment.

We finished dinner without further incident. I got up from the table with everyone else, and Mr. Pinkam approached me with that look back on his face. "I would like to have a word in private with you young man. Follow me.", as he led me into the living room where he grabbed a Bible off of a shelf and slammed it into my hand.

"I want you to go into your bedroom and read this." I looked up at him like he was nuts and said, "Why would I want to read this? I am not religious!", without giving him the chance to answer I continued, "Where is the TV?"

That was it. That did it. The other side of him unleashed like a lion in the wild. He pointed and screamed, "You will take this book, and you will read it until I tell you that you can stop." He grabbed me by the ear and dragged me through the living room, dining room, and on to the rec room, where he let go and pointed toward my bedroom, "Get in there!"

I stood for a second and looked at him with daring eyes. Go ahead Mister, Smack me! I didn't want him to dislike me, I wanted him to HATE me. I wanted him to pick up the phone and call someone to come and get me. Once again, he baffled me. Crouching down to my height, he whispered in my ear;

"Listen, I realize that you haven't had it that easy. Otherwise you wouldn't be here.", pausing to rub the sandpapered stubble on his chin, "But in my house, you will live by rules. Do you understand?"

What was I supposed to do? I just shrugged my shoulders and said yes. He looked at me deeply, and the dark and secret wielding look was gone, replaced by a concerned one. "I only want to help you. So just go on to your room while I get your stuff settled. OK? Don't worry about the reading. We'll do it another time.", as he gave me a slight grin.

I stared my blank stare at him for a second, and walked into the bedroom and softly pulled the door shut. Looking around the room, I sighed. How did I get here? I had so many questions and nobody could answer them. I plopped down onto the bed and closed my eyes to try to avoid the tears that were coming. I wanted my dad. Even with as mad and confused as I was, one thing was plain; I wanted my dad.

As I was in my tearful rest, Mr. Pinkam was in the living room giving my belongings a thorough inspection for contraband. I tried to make myself a mental picture of what could be in there that he might disapprove of. I didn't have any weed left from my morning house parties. Mostly G.I. Joes and Transformers. The only thing that I could think of would be that some of the comic books were perhaps a little too gory. Let's see, I thought, is there anything else? Just as I began to ponder that, there was a knock at the door.

Peeking her head inside my room, Mrs. Pinkam looked at me through the shadow casted from the setting sun. "Steven, honey, can you come into the kitchen? My husband and I would like to have a little talk with you.", she gave me a warm smile, "Come on dear, it's ok."

She could see from my glazed eyes that I had been crying. I was ashamed of my tear stained face. My nose crusted with snot, I looked away from her. "I don't want to talk, I want to go home, I'm scared."

"Oh you poor dear.", she said softly as she came in and sat down on the bed. "Come here.", grabbing me and holding me to her heart. I could smell the fruity scent of her soap. The beating of her heart comforted my ears with its steady rhythm, "I am so sorry that you are hurting dear. Please listen to me. We are going to take good care of you. You have nothing to be afraid of. You will be safe here.", stroking her fingers through my greasy hair.

Could it be that this family wasn't as bad as I thought they were? Were they just trying to help? My soul was tired. Every corner of my tattered heart ached with a pain that only death could bring. Not death in life, but the death of a part of me that I was trying so desperately to cling to. The death of my childhood.

I followed Mrs. Pinkam into the kitchen, where her husband was waiting for us. He could see from my defeated face that I was having a hard time adjusting. He stood up and put his hand on my shoulder, looking at his wife with concerned eyes.

"Jim, our new friend is having a bit of a rough time with this situation. Perhaps this isn't the best time to do this."

"Hmm-mm", clearing his throat, "Sure darling. Why don't you go and draw him a bath. This can wait.", winking at me, he smiled, "Go on with JoAnne, we'll finish this in the morning."

I followed her down the hallway and sat on the edge of the green tub while she poured a small amount of bubble bath into the steamy water. As the bubbles spread through the water, for the first time in days, I was relaxed.

After a long exchange about the house rules, I adjusted as well as I could to my new surroundings, and the second half of my summer went by rather quickly. I would spend my mornings doing household chores. My afternoons were filled by my classes at Vacation Bible School. Which was something that I was against, but did anyway. I never had a great interest in religion, but in this house, religion was a way of life. I had no choice. I caved into the rampant insistence of trying to 'Find Christ' and went along with the program that they had laid out for me. Bible school wasn't that bad. It was more of a day camp than a church thing. Gathering the kids of the parish together and helping us learn a little more about God. While entertaining our minds about theology, they also taught us other things. They taught me how to walk on stilts, I showed them how to ride a skateboard. They showed me how to pray, I showed them how to Yo-Yo. It was a fair exchange of knowledge. I even learned a passage from the Bible. Even now, decades later, I still remember that passage:

"For God so loved the world, that he gave his only begotten son. That whosoever believeith in him, shall not perish, but have everlasting life. For God sent not his son into the world to condemn the world, but that the world through him might be saved." JOHN 3:16-17

That passage never meant much to me. It still doesn't. I just remember having to learn it, and it has stuck with me ever since. I have always had a certain affliction toward religion. I am not exactly sure when it began. But it is still with me today. I don't have a problem with anyones choice to believe in something bigger than us. But it has never been for me. The fact that The Pinkam's were so religious might have fueled my desire to stay away from it, or perhaps, I just felt that I was so estranged from a normal life as a kid, that if there was indeed a God, he would have saved me from my misery. Either way, I am ok with my beliefs. Even if they don't go along with everyone else's.

As the summer came to an end, the sixth grade was looming in the distance. I had started to settle comfortably in my new surroundings. My foster parents were genuinely good people. I recognized this as they continued to care for me, in spite of my character. They got me new clothes for school, and even bought me a new bike to replace the one that I had left at my dad's house.

On the first day of school, I got on the bus for the five mile ride to Thompson Middle School. I walked into the building and found the office to check in. I really didn't know any of the kids in the school. There were a few on the bus that I remembered seeing as I was mowing the lawn during the summer. None of us had spoken though, so we were still strangers in the hallways. Passing glances on the way to and from classes. This was the first time that I had to switch classes for every class. It took a while to get used to. Having to pack up when the bell rang and try to find the next classroom before it rang again. The kids were mostly nice, and the teachers were very interested in actually making sure that the students were indeed learning.

I quickly adjusted to my new schedule and began to fraternize with the other kids. I met a kid named Justin and we became fast friends. Justin lived just a half block from the school, so I would often skip getting on the bus to go home, and just walk over to his house instead. We would hang out until his mother came home, and she would drive me back to the Pinkam's when it was time for me to go.

The first time that I didn't come straight home from school, Jim and JoAnne were a little worried about my absence. When I walked in the front door, they were waiting for me with discerning looks on their faces.

"Where were you? Why didn't you get on the bus and come home?", JoAnne exclaimed, "We were worried sick." Jim was just standing there in his best fatherly stance.

"I went to a friend's house.", looking up at them with a fearful look in my eyes. Were they going to try and make me read the Bible again?

"Oh." JoAnne exhaled, "That's okay. It's good that you are making friends.", she glanced over at her husband, who responded, "Next time just call and tell us where you are."

I continued my after school activities every day. Often on the weekends, Justin's mother would pick me up at my house and take us out to the mall or a movie. Justin and I spent a lot of time listening to music. He had a collection of tapes that rivaled any one that I had ever seen. One day Justin put on a Motley Crue tape and I just sat in awe as I heard the first song; "Shout at the Devil". We would sit and bang our heads back and forth the same way we had seen bands on MTV do it. He loaned me the tape to take home and listen to. A mistake that I would come to regret.

The Pinkam's had tried their best with me. They had been patient and loving. Even though at times, I bucked at their rules and did my own thing, they remained true to my cause. But, one day when JoAnne was cleaning my room, something happened that was the last straw. I came home from school one day to find her sitting in the living room with a look that can only be described as frightened. Her eyes stared at me like I was the spawn of a demon.

"You need to go to your room and not come out until Jim comes home.", pointing toward the right side of the house.

"What's wrong? What did I do?", I asked in confusion.

"Just go to your room and don't say another word!", she sternly said with a tone to rival a priest who was trying to exorcise an evil spirit from a damned soul, "GO, NOW!", she grunted.

I went to my room without further discussion and waited to find out what I had done wrong. What could it be that had her so mad I wondered. Did a teacher call her and say something bad? Did my dad call her and tell her something about my past that she couldn't accept?

I soon found out that it was neither of those things. Jim came to my door and looked deep into my eyes. The warm and patient look that I had come to know from him during these past few months was gone. Replaced now with a look of total defiance. "Come with me right now.", inhaling in short bursts like a lifelong smoker breathing through an oxygen mask. "We NEED to talk!"

Confused, I got up and followed him out to the kitchen to see what I had done. I walked in to find JoAnne sitting at the table in tears. Raising her head, her teary eyes cried out at me, "Haven't we been good to you? Haven't we tried to help you in your time of need?", holding up the Motley Crue tape in her tightly clenched hand, "and this is how you repay us?", slamming the tape on the table. "This is how you show your appreciation?"

"It's just a tape.", I responded timidly, "I didn't mean anything by it. It's just music.", looking at both of them like I was about to be executed.

Jim sat down next to me. His hands clenched into fists, he placed them firmly on the table. "Do you have any idea what this music does to kids your age?"

"Nothing!", I proclaimed, "It's just music!", I looked at both of them like I was a child caught stealing a chocolate bar, and they were the owners of the store.

"This music is the work of the Devil.", Jim shouted, "I will not have it in my house. Do you understand me?", JoAnne sat there and looked into my eyes deeply for a hint of understanding.

"I'm sorry! I didn't mean anything by it.", answering in fright.

"Tell us where you got it.", JoAnne demanded. "It was that kid that you are always with after school, wasn't it?", she paused to remember his name, "It was this Justin.", looking at her husband. "We should call his mother.", she stated plainly.

I just sat there. I understood that they were a very religious family, but it was just a tape. It wasn't like I had satanic images etched into my skull. It was just some music. What was the big deal? I didn't know what to do. I didn't know what to say. I just sat there waiting for one of them to say something, anything. They just stared at me.

They would avert their eyes for a second and look at each other. Then they would just stare back at me with empty, defeated eyes.

"We are going to have to figure this whole thing out before we can determine what to do about it.", Jim said in monotone, "For now, I just want you to stay in the house. You are to go to school and then come straight home afterwards. Do you understand Son?", he questioned.

"Yes Sir, but please, I wasn't trying to be bad. It's just music.", pausing for a second to figure out my next words. "Please don't be mad at me. I didn't mean anything by it.", scared of what they would do.

"We will figure it out. Don't worry Son.", his voice said that he was understanding, but his eyes showed that he was afraid of me. I was a ten year old kid, why should he be afraid of me?

I went to my room to relax, and slept right through dinner. The next morning I got up and went to school without a word. There was a tension in the air for the next twenty four hours, but nothing else was mentioned about my devilish deed. My eleventh birthday was just three days away. I hoped the matter would be settled before then. I hoped that they would forgive me.

December 16, 1986 started out like a normal day. Only this was the day I turned eleven years old. I was awakened with a birthday greeting from Mrs. Pinkam.

"Wake up Steven, Happy Birthday!!", she crooned as I rubbed the grit out of my eyes.

I smiled and politely said, "Thank You!", sitting up to look out the window for the expected snowfall. "What time is it?"

"It's almost seven thirty. You've got to get ready for school. So let's go, Up and at 'em!", she lightly swatted my behind in jest.

A smile came to my face as I walked toward the bathroom to wash up before school. Things are going to be ok, I thought. After my morning ritual of a shower and breakfast, I was off to school. The bus ride was pleasant, I sat there looking out the window imagining the birthday presents that would be awaiting me when I got home that afternoon. I pictured the birthday cake with eleven big candles, glowing with the intensity of an eternal flame. I imagined that they would all be waiting for me in the living room clapping and shouting at my arrival. Yelling out at me, "Happy Birthday!" I pictured a big and brightly colored banner to announce my special day.

Unbeknownst to me at the time, although they would be waiting for me in the living room, it wouldn't be for a birthday celebration. It would be to wish me goodbye.

When I arrived back at the house after school, Jim and JoAnne were waiting for me in the living room. Sitting on the couch next to them was the caseworker who had dropped me off at their house just six months before.

"What's going on?", I asked, surveying the room. No birthday banner, no cake, no celebration at all. The woman on the couch stood up and reached out her hand.

"Steven, do you remember me? I am Mrs. Andrews, we met a few months ago when I brought you here.", she looked like she had just committed a crime. Her eyes told the task that she was about to perform.

I ran to the back of the house and locked myself in my room. She had come to take me away. Only now, I didn't want to leave. I wanted to stay. A knock came at the door, and when I opened it, the caseworker was there. I wanted to ask what was happening, but I didn't. I just hugged her. She returned my embrace. Whispering in my ear softly.

"Come on kiddo, let's get your stuff together. I will take you to dinner since it's your birthday. I will explain all of this to you. Come on.", with the softness of a newly bought sweater.

After taking me out to eat at Sizzler, and explaining to me that The Pinkam's couldn't look after me anymore, Mrs. Andrews brought me to meet my new family. While we were eating, she assured me the main problem with Jim and JoAnne was not me, it was them. They had felt that they just weren't capable of handling another child, on top of the three that they already had. Although she said that it wasn't my fault, I knew better. They had given up on me just like everyone else had. Maybe it was the Motley Crue tape. I suspected that it was more than that. Although I wasn't sure what else it could be.

ZEM.TC4

e:	Modern Day Orphan: How A Boy Lost His Way
nd:	Very Good
er:	on_lister1
tion:	ZB-01
te:	2024-08-02 20:51:11 (UTC)
count:	Zoom Books East
ig Loc:	Small 7-Bay 7-Shelf 1
SKU:	ZEM.TC4
KU:	ZEV.B0BRDFLJSR.VG
eq#:	257
it_id:	17139039
dth:	0.79 in
nk:	2,424,960

ZEV.B0BRDFLJSR.VG

delist unit# 17139039

xxxxx

ZEM TCA

Modern Day Orphan, How A Boy
Lost His Way
Very Good
on_listen1
ZB-01
2024-08-02 20:51:11 (UTC)
Zoom Books East
Small 7-Bay 7-Shelf 1
ZEM-TC4
ZEV BOBRDFL1SR VG
257
17139039
0.79 in
2,424.880

ZEV BOBRDFL1SR VG

delist unit# 17139039

xxxxx

THE RENRICK RESIDENCE
EAST KEANSBURG, NJ
DECEMBER 1986

This was to be my new home? This split level house that reeked of cat piss? The woman who came to the door had to weigh at least two hundred seventy pounds. Her husband in his crusty flannel shirt had her beat by at least fifty more. As the kids ran by me, I lost track of just how many there were. I counted four, but it seemed like there were many, many more.

Mrs. Andrews introduced me to the burly couple, "Steven, this is Mrs. Renrick.", who extended a set of plump fingers stretched out from her arm like an assortment of donuts.

"Nice to meet you….Steven?, is it?", engulfing my tiny hand in her grasp. "This is my husband Al.".

The man stepped forward, wiping off his greasy hands on the flannel before reaching out for mine. "Hey, how are ya?", he grumbled, his hot breath stinking of a three day drinking binge.

"Hi", I answered, shaking his hand as he tightened his grip, "Nice to meet you.", my bones rubbing at each other like two sticks trying to start a fire.

"Well, I'm not sure how long you're gonna be with us, but let's get you a bunk to sleep in.", the stout man said as he led me down the hallway toward what seemed like a large dormitory.

Mrs. Andrews had explained to me over dinner that I would only be staying here temporarily until they could find me a more permanent home. "It might be a week, it might be a month."

The large room had four sets of bunk beds. Each with its own set of shelves on the wall next to it. Toys were scattered around all over. I had to watch my step as I walked behind Mr. Renrick to my new 'room'. A huge step downward from the last one. He pointed to a bunk, and grumbled "There ya go, get settled, and I will catch ya later." as he walked out the door. I climbed the ladder and sat down on the rickety bunk bed.

"How long are you gonna be here?", a voice squeaked from the corner of the room. I looked to see where it came from and saw a kid who looked about two years older than me hunkered down behind a dresser. His head was sticking out from the side, "Hey kid, didn't you hear me? How long?"

I don't know.", unimpressed by his fake tough attitude. "Probably just for a week or two, until I get a new foster family."

"Yeah, sure. That's what they told me too.", as he jumped out of his hiding place, "Know how long ago that was?"

"How long ago?", I firmly asked. I wasn't sure what he was going to say, but I was sure that I would not like the answer too much.

"Six years ago!", he aptly stated, "Six years!", counting his fingers out, "One, Two, Three, Four, Five, Six long years!", waiting for my reaction.

"Well, I won't be here THAT long!", I fed right into his invitation, "I'll be back with my real family by then.", my face grimaced with hope.

He laughed in my face, "Ha! Gotcha!", holding his stomach , "I'm Jack.", grinning from ear to ear he continued, "I'm not a foster kid."

"So, those are your real parents?", I asked, pointing towards the door.

"Yeah, have been since birth.", he strutted for the door, his voice trailing, "Come on, I'll show you around. Follow me." as he started to run down the hallway.

I followed him down the hallway as he pointed out the kitchen, and the bathroom. "Over here is the door to the family room downstairs.", he pointed at a door as he ran past it. There were kids scattered here and there as I followed him through a maze of rooms. The other kids varied in age, but all of them seemed younger than I was by at least five years.

Once we were back in the kitchen, Jack offered me a Coke and took me downstairs to the family room. "Where were you living before?", he asked as he was fumbling with the TV remote.

"Middletown. Do you know where that is?", I asked. I was wondering just what town I was in now.

"Sure, it's only two towns over from here. What school did you go to there? Thompson?", he inquired.

"Yeah, but only since September. Before that I lived up North.", offering more than he asked.

Jack looked right at me with his gap teeth, "Well, now you're going to have to go to Thorne Middle School. Trust me, you'll hate it. They kept me back twice."

"What grade are you in?", I asked, not exactly sure just how old he was.

"I'm in the sixth, but I am supposed to be in the eighth.", he snorted, "How 'bout you?"

"Sixth too.", I responded.

Jack went on to tell me that he was thirteen. He also told me about the various house rules. Don't touch ANYTHING in the upstairs living room. Don't go into the garage, and "Whatever you do, NEVER go into my parents bedroom!", he said with the most serious look I had ever seen on a kid's face, "They do not allow that."

A few days later, I started at my new school. Jack was right, I hated it. The teachers were boring, and they didn't seem to care if we were paying attention or not. I tried to be attentive to their teaching. But I just couldn't stay interested in the dull voices ringing from their mouths.

With Christmas just days away, my mother phoned Renrick's to offer to take me over to her house from the 23rd until New Years Day. The Renrick's asked me and I was ecstatic. I couldn't believe that mom wanted me to visit.

"Really? She wants me to stay with her?", I asked as I hoped that I could convince her to keep me forever and never send me back to foster care. I had to try to make her want me back.

Mom picked me up as planned. During the ride, she seemed nervous. I assumed that she was afraid of asking me about my 'new life', so I offered;

"I don't like my new school Mom. The teachers are boring.", giving her an opening, which she easily took.

"Well, sometimes teachers can be like that. You have to pay attention so you can learn though", her knuckles white as she gripped the steering wheel tightly. "How about the new house? How's that going?"

What should I say? I wondered. If I told her that I liked it, then she definitely wouldn't take me for good. If I told her that I hated it, she would just think that I was being dramatic and wouldn't take me either.

"I'm not sure yet Mom.", trying to throw her for a loop, "I'm really not sure."

I was going to make her want me. I'd behave better than I ever had before. I'd walk the dog. I'd do the dishes. I'd even take out the trash. She would give in. I would see to that.

Christmas came and went without incident. I was the epitome of a perfect child. There were no arguments with my stepfather David. I didn't have to be asked to do anything. I volunteered for all of the chores that needed to be done in the house. Leaving my brother and sister free to enjoy their holidays.

Mom seemed happy to have me around, if only briefly. My grandparents were down at mom's for a few days and they seemed happy to see me as well. I tried to do everything that was necessary to ensure my goal of being able to stay.

When New Year's Day came, I was dreading going back to the Renrick's. Mom came into the room as I was laying in the bed and sat down next to me.

"Steven", she said as she stroked my head, "I know that all of this is hard for you..", pausing to take a deep breath, "But I really don't know what to do for you.", Her eyes said that she was sorry for the things that happened, but behind them I could see that she wasn't going to take me in.

"Mom, why can't I stay here with you? I will be good.", I tried to reason with her, "I don't want to go back to that place.", with pools of saline filling my eyes, "I want to be here with you. Please don't make me go back!", sitting up to embrace her tightly, "Please don't make me go back.", I whispered in her ear. She gripped me tight and I could hear her mild sobbing, and shallow breathing. With her arms tightly around me, she exhaled,

"I don't know what to do. David doesn't want you here, and I don't want to ruin what I have here with him.", she seemed frail as newly sheeted ice as she hugged me.

"Can't you talk to him Mom? Can't you explain that I will be good? Just give me a chance. Tell him to give me a chance.", the snot dripping from my nose as I shuddered at the thought of having to leave.

Mom pulled back from my grip and looked me square in the eyes, "I will see what I can do, but for now, you have to go back. Maybe we can find a way to work this out, okay?", as her hand brushed across my tearful stained cheeks.

I nodded, and snorted, "OK Mom, just don't forget about me. Don't forget where I am.", looking at her with the eyes of a lost puppy, "Don't forget about me."

After saying my goodbye to Nicole and Robert, Mom and I got in the car for the ride back to East Keansburg.

She really didn't say much in the car. Like the ride down, she once again seemed afraid to comment on anything. I took her silence with a grain of salt and chose to stare out the window at passing cars and the tired faces of toll booth attendants as they collected change. I could only live with the hope that my mom's plea for me would work. The hope that my life would become normal again. The hope that I could live in a home where I could be happy without the fear of someone coming to take me away at any moment. Where someone wouldn't abandon me at the first sign of trouble. I would try to do whatever was necessary for me to get it.

My return to the Renrick's was uneventful. Mom walked me to the door and gave me a hug and kiss. She told me that she would see me as soon as she could, reminded me to behave and left. Watching her car slowly bounce down the snow covered road, it occurred to me that I was once again alone. No matter how many children were here with me, I was by myself in this fight. There was no one to help me in my quest. Just me.

Less than two weeks later, Mrs. Andrews was back to pick me up and take me to yet another new home. When the doorbell chimed, and she walked in the front door, I was actually happy to see her. I wanted to get out of there.

As we loaded my things into the back of her state-issued Dodge, I asked her enthusiastically, "Mrs. Andrews, Mrs. Andrews, what is my new home going to be like?", tugging at her winter coat, "Mrs. Andrews…", she cut me off from my pestering.

"Please Steven, call me Carol.", she squatted down to my level, "I think that we know each other well enough now to be on a first name basis, so call me Carol. Go on and get into the car and I will explain everything when we are on the road.", smiling at me like a loving aunt.

I didn't really want to say goodbye to anyone in the Renrick's house and they didn't seem eager to come out and wish me off either. So I got into the front seat and waited for Carol to start the car. As we headed down the road, she turned down the radio and said to me,

"This new home is a little bit different. Instead of living with a whole family, it's just going to be you, your new foster mom Renee and her roommate Jean.", she winked at me coyly, "You don't have to worry about any other kids running around trying to steal your thunder."

I thought about it for a second. Picturing what it would be like to be an only child again. I imagined that it would be similar to the way it was with me and my dad. Only this time I figured that no one would come and drag one of us away in handcuffs.

"Where does Renee live?" I asked, "What is she like?", not giving her a chance to answer. "What is Jean like?" I kept on asking question after question. Carol just smiled and waited for me to let her have a word.

"Renee is a great woman, and so is Jean", once I gave her an opportunity to answer, "They live in a small house in Bradley Beach, just three blocks from the ocean." I just smiled, thinking about living by the beach again. "You like the ocean, don't you Steven?", She asked.

"I love it!", excited at the news, "When I lived in San Diego I lived just a few blocks from the beach too!" I sat back in my seat and tried to imagine what my new life would be like. Surely it had to be better than the last month living with a half a dozen kids and two 'parents' who were only interested in the financial aspects of looking after foster kids. This would be different. I just knew it.

RENEE TAYLOR'S HOUSE
BRADLEY BEACH, NJ
JANUARY 1987

It was a small two story blue clapboard house with white trim crammed in between two other houses. The front had a small sun porch with the shades pulled down. On the second floor was a balcony with a set of wind chimes blowing in the crisp winter air. I looked up and exhaled. The warm vapor burst from my lips. This might actually be ok, I thought.

"Hello, My name is Renee.", the young woman smiled. Her short blond hair curled around the bottom of her ears. "This is my roommate Jean.", nodding toward the dark haired woman sitting on the couch who grinned at me like a young school girl with a crush. "You must be Steven.", Renee said in a soft voice, "It's great to finally meet you. We've heard so much about you." Jean stood up and approached me, "Yes, we have been looking forward to your arrival.", giving my shoulder a little squeeze, "We're glad you are going to be staying here with us.", once again grinning at me.

I'm not sure just how old these women were, but they were definitely younger than both of my parents were. They seemed to be like two sisters in their first home away from their parents house. Renee had a thin tone to her that showed she kept in shape. She was only about five foot three, and had the face of an angel. Jean was about the same height with a similar build, but her chest was a lot bigger than Renee's was. She reminded me of someone I had seen on television once. They seemed like a nice pair of parents, but I just couldn't get past just how young they seemed to be. Maybe it was because I had envisioned all foster parents to be older and out of shape. These women were different. That much was very clear to me.

I got a short tour of the house. Living room, kitchen, sun porch, bathroom downstairs. Upstairs, Renee's bedroom was the largest. She had the balcony. Right next to hers was Jean's, and on the opposite of the stairs was my room and a spare room which was empty. The walls of the house were adorned with photographs of women running and jumping on the beach, or smiling at the camera while sitting on lawn chairs. The pale green carpet was freshly vacuumed and the air smelled of strawberries. I just smiled from ear to ear as they showed me around. It was very cozy. There were bookshelves in every room, each stuffed with novels and photo albums.

Renee taught the third grade at a school in Roselle, NJ. Which was about a forty five minute drive north. Roselle was only about ten miles from Hillside where I lived before. She told me that I was going to be enrolled at the school she taught at, so we would drive up together every morning.

"That way you can be right near me if you need me.", she stated in a way that showed interest in my well being, "I'll just be a few classrooms down the hall.", showing her comforting grin again.

Jean was a clerk of some sort who worked in the county courthouse. She really didn't say a lot at first. Just sat by idly as Renee talked with me. Jean seemed pleased to have me around, but Renee was excited about my arrival.

"If you want..", Renee said hurriedly, "we can go out and get you some new clothes for your new school. I know that Christmas just passed and I understand that you recently had a birthday."

"Yeah.", I responded to her offer, "My birthday was last month, December 16th.", I smiled as she looked at me with tender blue eyes. This was great. She was going to take me shopping. The first day in her home she wanted to take me shopping for new clothes!

"Is there anything else that you want to buy besides clothes? Are you interested in any books or…", pausing to think for a second, then snapping her fingers like she had just solved a mystery, "..Are you into art? Do you like to draw? We can get you some drawing stuff too if you like.", she pointed at Jean, "Jean here is quite an artist, maybe she can show you some stuff."

"Sure that would be great!", I tried to be as polite as I could be so I could make a good impression, "I used to draw a little bit."

Renee gave me a tight hug, "So, it's settled then, we are going shopping!", she let out a little grunt as she hugged me, pinched me and said, "You are such an handsome little devil.", looking over at Jean, she asked, "Jean, isn't he the cutest kid that you've ever seen?"

"He's adorable..", stopping for a second, then looking right at me, "You are adorable.", standing up, she said, "Come on and give us a hug." The three of us hugged for a minute before Renee jumped up and shouted, "Let's get out of here and do some shopping!", grabbing her coat off the wooden rack by the door, "We should probably go and get a bite to eat first.", She zipped up my coat and asked, "What do you want for lunch little man?", adjusting my collar, "We can go anywhere you like, you name it."

"How about pizza?", hoping that it was ok, I asked with a little bit of hesitance. I clearly wasn't used to having so many options. This was all so new to me. I knew one thing though, I wasn't going to be eating whole wheat spaghetti!

"Pizza it is! Come on let's go.", putting one hand in mine and the other in Jean's, we walked off to the car for our day of fun.

We had lunch and went shopping at the Monmouth Mall. One of the malls that I used to spend Nikki's money at. They bought me a bunch of new clothes and some new sneakers. Then we went to an art supply store where Renee and Jean filled a cart with pads of drawing paper of various sizes, paints, brushes, pens, pencils and markers. They wanted to make sure that I had enough stuff to keep me busy. I just nodded yes to everything that they held up and asked if I wanted.

That was the way it was for the three of us. We were like three friends just living in the world without a care. Pretty soon I forgot about my own cares, and settled into my life. I started at my new school and was content with the rush-hour drive every morning. Normally the drive would take less than an hour. However, most days it took more than an hour with the morning traffic. Every morning, when we got off the Parkway at the Roselle exit, we would stop at Dunkin Donuts for breakfast. The first time we went in for breakfast, the old woman at the counter said to Renee as she poured the coffee,

"Renee, who is this young man? One of your students?", she smiled with a grandmother's grin.

"Trudy, this is Steven. My new Son!", as she always introduced me. She never used the word 'Foster'. She didn't seem to like it, and she somehow knew that I didn't either. "Steven, this is Trudy.", pointing at the counter.

"Hi!, nice to meet you Ma'am.", I responded in my best manners. Trudy looked down at me from the high counter and said,

"It's a pleasure to meet you. What would you like to have this morning?" Her eyes lit up, "Oh, I know! How about a cup of hot chocolate and donut?", she looked at Renee for her approval and she nodded yes, "What kind of donut?"

"Jelly Please!", I exclaimed. "Thank you!"

That was our morning routine. Each day Trudy would have our breakfast waiting for us as we pulled into the parking lot. I looked forward to our morning breakfast as we headed off to school together. We'd sit and chat while we ate. It was nice to be welcomed in the morning. It was a pleasant feeling to be accepted.

The next few months flew by, and before I knew it, the snow was gone and the flowers were in full bloom. I went to school everyday with Renee and, with the exception of a few normal childhood quarrels with some of the other kids, all was well. Jean and I would spend our evenings watching TV while Renee graded schoolwork. The only thing that Renee was strict about was that I wasn't allowed to watch TV until I finished my homework. Which I couldn't get around anyway, since she worked at the school.

Little by little I started to spend time at mom's house. First just an afternoon at a time. Then a few weekends here and there. As Summer was coming, I looked forward to a break from school.

One day, when Renee had to go up to school for a conference, I got to stay home and relax. Jean had to work since it was a weekday, so they agreed that I would fine by myself for the day. They trusted that I wouldn't get into any trouble while I was gone. Renee would call the house every once in a while to make sure I was okay. I decided that I would snoop around a little bit while they were gone. As I poured through the photo albums on the bookshelves, and stared at all of the pictures of women on the walls, something occurred to me. There were never any men in this house. Neither Renee or Jean had a boyfriend over. While pondering this, I came across an envelope of pictures behind some books. When I opened the envelope, I couldn't believe my eyes. There were naked photos of Renee and Jean together kissing each other in the living room and out in the grass behind the house. There were pictures of other women, just as naked, doing even more than kissing. Among the photos were a few women lined up in a row, completely nude and holding up signs that said things like 'Sweet Pussy', and 'Hot Momma'. It looked like some sort of naked dating game or charades. I was astounded. It finally occurred to me that the reason there was never any men around was that they were lesbians. Even though I wasn't even twelve years old yet, I KNEW what a lesbian was. I had seen all sorts of these things in magazines and movies, but this was different. This was the real thing. All of a sudden, the mild, crush-like attraction I had to Renee was amplified by ten. No longer would I have to imagine what she looked like naked as I laid in bed at night masturbating. I had pictures. I decided to hide the pictures beneath my mattress for later viewing and went back to my search for more things. My search was fruitless.

When Renee came home, I saw her in a completely different light. She had no idea of my discovery, so I tried to maintain my normal behavior. Jean and I would cuddle on the couch at night watching TV as usual. Only now, I knew their little secret. They were a lesbian couple who obviously could not have a kid of their own. Back then, it wasn't a normal thing for a gay couple to adopt a child, as it is today. So they instead opted to take a kid that needed a home. That was fine with me. I was just happy to be wanted by someone, anyone! I don't want to paint them like they were some sort of deviants, because they were not. They were always good to me. Never once did either of them treat me badly, and they never exposed me to the private world that they lived in.

My weekend visits with mom became a weekly thing. The plan, as it was put to me by Renee and Mrs. Andrews, was to have me living with my mom by the time school started up again in the Fall. I'm not exactly sure if it was just their plan, or if my mom and David were a part of it too. The only thing I knew was that although I was content to be where I was, I wanted my family back even more.

It was during one of my weekend visits to mom's house that everything changed for me. David and I had gotten into a little argument that escalated when he hit my little brother for doing something wrong. I couldn't deal with that, so I threw my radio at him in defense of my brother.

The next thing I knew, Renee was picking me up and we were driving back to Bradley Beach. Although she seemed a little upset at my behavior, her voice had a concerned tone to it when she asked,

"Steven, baby, I don't understand why you would do something like that. Don't you want to go back with your family?", she questioned my actions, "Do you want to stay with us? Tell me what you want.", as she steered the car down the road. Confused by what had happened.

"I love staying with you guys. I really do!", and I really did, "But sometimes I'm not sure what I really want.", I looked over at her, "I don't know what I want.", I said sheepishly.

"Well, maybe we should find you someone to talk about your feelings with honey.", she smiled, "I will call Carol and we will find someone to help you work through it."

I started to cry. I just knew she was giving up on me. She wasn't though. She really did want me around. I think that deep down, she didn't want me to go back to live with my family.

"We'll get through this. You and me kiddo", she grabbed my hand, "I will call Carol tomorrow, and we will work it out together."

The best course of action was decided for me to have a mental health evaluation. I really wasn't sure what that was, but I went along with it. A few days later, Carol came to pick Renee and I up and took us to Piscataway. Which was about halfway between where we lived and school. I was to spend the afternoon talking to a doctor about my feelings. My mother and David were supposed to be there as well. That way we could all talk out our issues with each other. As the car headed North, I hoped that I could make a good impression on the Doctor. Renee, in her comforting voice offered,

"Maybe he can help you better understand why you have been through some of the things that you have been through", She knew that I was scared of going, but her nature was supportive. "You'll be fine", she stated, "After we are done, we can go back to the house and take a walk to the beach.", smiling that soft smile. Little did I know at the time, I would never step foot in Renee's house again.

COMMUNITY MENTAL HEALTH CENTER
PISCATAWAY, NEW JERSEY
JUNE 1987

The Community Mental Health Center was a division of Rutgers University in Piscataway. Just a few miles from Rutgers main campus in New Brunswick. The brick building was long and large, with grassy hills on both sides. As we walked inside, I saw the directory on the wall, which had so many names, numbers and departments listed.

The three of us met up with Mom and David, and we all approached the reception together. We were directed to the elevator and instructed to go to the third floor. None of us spoke on the ride upstairs. Mom was shifting her weight from side to side, in her best attempt to seem like she was in a good mood. David stood there stone faced and stared straight ahead. Carol clutched her thick folder to her chest, and Renee gripped my hand tightly as she smiled down at me with a look that said: 'Everything is going to be just fine'. My heart was pounding as the door slid open and we stepped out to determine the root of my problems.

After checking in with another receptionist, we were directed to a waiting area. The five of us divided ourselves into separate groups, with Mom and David sitting on one side, and the rest of us on the other side. After a few minutes of waiting, a man in a well tailored suit came through a door and approached us.

Looking around at the bunch, he shifted his eyes in my direction and said, "You must be Steven.", holding out his hand, "I am Doctor Warner.", trying his best to force a smile. "Why don't we go and have a little talk, shall we."

I looked at Renee, and she nodded at me to let me know that it would be okay. Once I got the approval I was seeking, I stood up and followed Dr. Warner down the hall to his stately office. Just like the office that I had been to in the Family Services building, this one too had wood paneled walls with a bunch of plaques and diplomas scattered about. I took a seat as he pointed to a chair and tried to relax. The Doctor followed suit and plopped himself behind the large oak desk scattered with files. Staring across the desk, he cleared his throat and said in a gruff voice,

"Do you know why you are here Steven?", his eyes looking right into mine without blinking.

"Yes, I am here to talk to you about my problems.", trying to tell him what I thought he wanted to hear, "I've got a lot of problems with my life right now and I am here to get you to help me understand them.", I paused, "Right?", trying to determine if that was the reason I was here.

"Well, you are about half correct. You are here for a psychiatric evaluation to determine the reasons you do some of the things you do.", he leaned forward and I could smell the coffee on his breath, "Do you understand?"

I wasn't sure what he had meant, but I looked at him and responded, "Yes, I understand."

"Good, now tell me about your life. Where did you grow up?", he inquired, seemingly curious about what my response would be.

"What do you want to know?", I asked back, "Where should I start off?", I wasn't really sure what he wanted to know.

"Start off with the earliest memory that you have and then go on from there.", giving me a slight wink. I raised my eyebrow and processed his request as I started to tell him my whole story. I told him about everything. My dad, San Diego, Nikki, my mom, the foster homes, Renee, everything that had happened to me for as long as I could remember.

While I rambled on about my past, he jotted things down on a notepad, and occasionally interrupted my confessions with, "Tell me a little more about that.", or "And how did that make you feel?", I would go on to answer his inquiries, and he would go back to his pen and pad.

After I relayed my entire existence to him, he was quiet for a minute. He looked down at me with his brown spotted hands crossed like a school boy, and all of a sudden he asked me,

"Do you ever hear voices? I mean besides the voices that come from people talking to you. People that you can see. Do you ever hear voices in your head?", not taking his eyes from mine.

What did he mean? I closed my eyes and could not think of the right answer. Sure, I heard voices. I could think back to the past and recall conversations that I had with people in the past, and in my head, I could hear what they had said. I could hear my dad screaming at me, or the words to a song that I liked. That had to be what he was talking about wasn't it? So, yes, I heard voices sometimes in my head. I opened my eyes and just blurted out,

"Of course I hear voices, doesn't everybody?", hoping that my answer was right and I would pass the test that he seemed to be giving me.

"That's interesting.", was the only response he had to offer to my answer. He looked down at his desk, wrote something down with his pen and stood up, "Why don't we take a little break. You can go out and wait with your family while I talk to your caseworker.", shuffling me toward the door.

I went back and just sat down with Renee. Meanwhile, my Mom and David joined Carol in the Doctor's office. I wondered what they were talking about in there. Sitting with Renee's arm around my shoulder, I looked up and asked,

"What do you think they are doing in there?", my curiosity getting the best of me.

"Oh, they are probably just having a chat. I wouldn't work about it. We should be out of here soon.", offering her usual comforting grin.

"Yeah, you're probably right.", I replied, glad that she was there with me. "Everything is going to be ok. Right Renee?", I looked at her deeply. She just continued smiling at me with those soft blue eyes.

"Of course it is sweetie, Of course!", giving my shoulder a squeeze. I smiled back up at her with the thought of going back to our little beach house.

A little while later, Mom, David, Carol and Dr. Warner came out of the office and came up to us. Mom looked like she had just seen a ghost. David was his usual self.

Carol looked worried. I took one look at them and stood up, approaching Carol,

"What's wrong Carol?", scared of her reply, "Did I pass the test?", knowing full well that I had done my best to answer all of the questions asked of me.

Renee stood up and placed herself between Carol and I and asked, "What's going on?", with the tone of a disciplinarian, "What are they going to do to him?", she knew that something wasn't right.

"Give us a minute Renee.", nodding down toward me, "Steven and I have to talk for a minute.", Renee parted from between Carol and I and looked at me with eyes that told me that everything WASN'T going to be okay.

Carol crouched down, and looked right into my eyes deeply before speaking, "Steven, I want you to listen to me very carefully. Do you understand?", I nodded, "The Doctor feels that you should stay here for a while so they can help you.", as the tears were welling up in my eyes, she continued, "Do you know what that means?"

I didn't get it. I answered his questions. I wasn't rude to him. Why did he want me to stay here? Why couldn't I leave with Renee? I didn't wait around to find out. I took off down the hallway screaming. Trying to find a door that would lead me back downstairs. Every door I approached was locked. I ducked into a bathroom and started to kick the stall door. I kicked it harder than I had kicked anything before in my life.

The noise must have given away my hiding place. Before I knew it, there were a bunch of people in the bathroom with me. One guy grabbed me and another stood between him and the door.

As I was screaming out, Renee came to the door and yelled out, "Steven Calm Down!", she looked at the man who was holding me, and said, "Give us a minute alone please.", he didn't budge. They stared at each other for a moment, and Renee screamed out at him, "Give us a minute! You can wait outside", pointing to the door. He shrugged and stepped out as Renee held me tightly.

"Listen honey, you have to go with these people. They can help you. Trust me, it's going to be okay.", she wiped the tears from my eyes and said, "I will come and visit you as soon as I can."

She kissed me and gave me another hug. We walked out of the bathroom together and before I knew it, she was gone. So were mom and David. I was alone again. Only this time I was locked behind the doors of a hospital wing. A psychiatric hospital from which I couldn't escape even if I wanted to.

ADOLESCENT IN-PATIENT UNIT: PISCATAWAY, NEW JERSEY
JUNE 1987

The Adolescent In-Patient Unit was a locked ward on the far side of the building. The walls were painted in calming tones. Every possible precaution had been taken to remove any dangerous furniture or times that may assist in damaging one's self. It was like a surreal dream, with all of the characters standing around with empty faces watching me be escorted through the buzzing doors.

My first twenty four hours upstairs were spent in an isolation room. I had to answer some routine questions that the nurses asked; Are you allergic to any medicine? Are you planning to hurt yourself or anyone else?, etc.. I just nodded no to their questions and sat on the bed staring off into oblivion like a catatonic. I heard everything they asked, but I didn't say a word for the first day. I was crushed by what had happened. I had lost my mom again, I had lost Renee. I was beginning to think that I had lost a part of myself as well. I wanted to cry, but the reservoirs in my eyes were empty. I couldn't shed a tear. I just sat there. My knees pulled to my chest, my arms hugging them. I was too confused to do anything else but sit there.

The next morning, a nurse came to the door and woke me out of my horrible slumber, "Wake up!", she lightly rapped on the door frame. "It's time for breakfast.", her voice raspy but gentle. "Come on, don't you want to eat? You've gotta eat something."

Sitting up, it took me a second to realize where I was. Apparently the whole thing wasn't a dream. I really was in this hospital. I stretched my arms, looked at the nurse with groggy eyes, "OK, I'm coming.", I stood up and followed her to the dayroom where there was a large metal cart with trays of food on it. As she pointed me to the food, I heard a voice behind me.

"The first three days, you've got to eat up here. After that, you get to go downstairs to the cafeteria." Turning around, I saw a girl behind me with burgundy hair that resembled the structure of a bird's nest. She smiled, following me as I got my tray. She seemed to be about three or four years older than me, but her eyes looked much older. I wondered what her story was. Was she lost too? I sat down at the table with her and she just looked across at me with wide eyes, not saying a word. Her mouth stuck in a permanent devious grin. I stared back. My own face returning her expression. "What?", I asked her.

"Oh, I'm sorry, I'm doing it again aren't I?", grabbing a handful of her messy hair with her fists, "I have a habit of staring at people.", she released her locks, "Aren't you gonna eat?", she nodded at my tray.

"I guess.", I grunted back. Looking at the breakfast of pancakes, sausage and pre-packaged cereal. "My name is Steve, what's yours?"

Well, STEVE..", she stated with eyes wide as an owl, "I am Susie, but everyone calls me Betty though.", she thrust her hand forward. As I shook it, she said, "It's a pleasure to meet you STEEEEVE.", enunciating my name with a very long E. She lowered her shoulders, and darted her eyes to the right and left, as if she was checking to see if anyone was watching, "Be careful, they're all nuts in here, but not me!", she proclaimed with a sheepish grin and owl eyes.

"What did you do to get in here?", I questioned, afraid of the answer that might come from her pursed lips.

"My dad used to beat me, so I tried to burn our house down.", her grin now wicked and glowing, "Then..", holding up her bandaged arms, "I slit my wrists so I could kill myself!"

"Oh!", not exactly sure how else to respond. I lowered my head to my tray and we had breakfast together without another word between us. When I was finished, I stood up and took the empty tray to the cart. Looking around me, I wasn't sure what to do next. Crazy eyed Betty walked over and grabbed my hand, "Come on!", pulling me toward the plastic couches where some of the other kids were sitting.

The majority of them looked like fairly normal kids. All of them were older than me. I didn't see one that was even close to my age. Some of them acknowledged me, some didn't. A few of them had weird smirks on their faces as they watched Betty and I plopping down on the couch. Betty's hands were locked into mine like a mother helping a child across the street.

"Everybody, this is STEEEEVE!", making a point to drag out the pronunciation of my name slowly, "STEEEEVE, this is everybody.", waving her arm around like a game show prize presenter. I just looked at them and mildly said, "Hi", as I waved my hand.

The next few days were a blur to me. I spent hours talking to Doctors. Answering questions that were repeated again and again, only in a different way each time. There were group meetings where everyone would stand up one at a time and introduce themselves, and say how they felt about this or that. At each meeting, Betty was right there next to me to make sure that I was ok. There were often screams coming from various rooms at different times of the day. I later found out that they were coming from what was known as the 'Quiet Room', which was a padded room with a half inflated soccer ball in it so you could kick it to get your frustrations out. Sometimes people would go into a quiet room voluntarily. At other times, they would be tackled by staff and literally be thrown into one.

A few times a day, everyone would line up at the nurses station for their assortment of medications. I wasn't one of the kids who were medicated, so I would just sit in the dayroom and watch them line up like homeless people waiting at a soup kitchen.

Before I knew it, a week had passed. I began to fall into a normal daily routine. Meals, group meetings, sessions with the Doctor, testing. Each day blended into the next like a merging intersection. Renee came up to see me one day and we sat in the dayroom and talked for a few hours about what it was like for me to be here. Seemed sad to see me locked up like some freak, but was supportive of my 'getting well'. Every few days, someone would freak out and try to commit suicide. They would try to cut themselves, or try to swallow a pencil. Some would even try to pound their heads into walls until they bled. Mostly, I was confused by this behavior. Sure, I had considered that dying would be better than the hell that I was enduring, but I never tried it. I was more shocked that my closest companion, Betty, who was clearly suicidal, had never once lost her cool. Even though she had previously wanted to die. Maybe the two of us were the only 'Normal' ones in there. Maybe everyone else was crazy and we were sane.

Life continued at a medium pace. There were more sessions with Doctors, tests with ink blots, and even an assortment of wires attached to my head to read my brainwaves, called an EEG. I went through the motions as they tried to determine the root of my actions.

Mom and David came up to the hospital a few times for family counseling meetings. The three of us would sit in a room for hours with a Doctor, discussing the different situations that we had been through in the past. The doctor mainly sat back as he posed questions to us to discuss amongst ourselves. When we were finished, he would usually follow up with, "and how does that make you feel?", or another abstract statement, "Tell me a little more about that."

All in all, I was just stagnant in my new surroundings. I kept quiet most of the time. I went to the meetings that I was supposed to. I didn't give the doctors a hard time. I just tried to behave. Every once in a while, I would volunteer to go into the quiet room and kick the soccer ball for a while. This was encouraged by the staff. They saw it as a way to keep us from bottling up our frustrations. They didn't want to have one of us snap out, although someone always did eventually. I just wanted to get out. I wanted to get back to my life. As my time in the unit was getting short, my companion, Betty got her own release. I was happy that she was leaving, but I must admit, I was sad to see her go. Betty gave me a big kiss goodbye and said to me,

"Goodbye sweet one, I have served my time.", she smiled her crazy grin, and handed me a piece of paper with an address, "Here, take this. It's my Grandma's house. I won't be there, but she will make sure that I get any messages."

Standing up, she went out the door and said, "Goodbye all you fuckers!", winked at me and was gone in the blink of an eye.

Not long after Betty's pardon, I was told that I would be leaving. I had been there for a total of six weeks. The Doctor called me into his office and asked me to sit down.

"Steven, you are leaving tomorrow. How do you feel about that?", chewing on the ends of his eyeglasses, "What are you going to do now that you are leaving?"

"I'm not really sure.", wondering just where I was going from here. "I guess my caseworker will take me back to live with my foster mom, Renee." At least that was what I assumed was going to happen.

The next day, just after lunch, I was called to the nurses station where there was a man waiting for me. The nurse looked at me and said, "Steven, this is John Wilkes from DYFS.", gesturing toward the bearded man in the cheap sport coat, "He is going to be taking you to your new placement."

I was confused, "Where is Carol Andrews?", I asked, pausing to think, "She is my caseworker. What do you mean by my new placement? Aren't I going back to Renee Taylor's?"

The man looked down at me and said with a grin, "Carol no longer works with DYFS", he put his hand on my shoulder and continued, "And No, you will not be going back there. We have a new placement for you."

The nurse handed him some paperwork, and he led me out of the hospital to the parking lot. As we got into his car, I asked "What do you mean by placement?, as I settled into the back seat. His response came out very slowly, "You'll see."

KILBARCHEN HOME FOR CHILDREN: PATERSON, NEW JERSEY JULY 1987

Mr. Wilkes didn't say a word during the one hour drive to Paterson. He just steered the car and listened to talk radio the whole way there. I just sat in the back with curiosity as to where we were going.

When we pulled into the parking lot, I knew that I was doomed. The building looked like an old school that had been shut down for decades. The brick and mortar had faded from years of the sun's abuse. At the corner of the parking lot was a basketball hoop with a rusty chain net hanging from it. Jumping around below it were a group of black kids of varying sizes. When they saw me get out of the car, they stopped and pointed. What was this place? I wondered. I knew that it wasn't a foster home. It surely wasn't another hospital. It looked like an orphanage.

My assumptions were close. It turned out that Kilbarchen used to be an orphanage. But with the advent of new agencies like DYFS, which were formed to help children in their time of need, the term orphanage went by the wayside years before. No matter what they called it, I knew what it was. To me, it was still an orphanage. I didn't want any part of it.

After walking me to the main office, the caseworker didn't stick around. He took my things out of the car, and brought them inside. Then he was gone, just as quietly as he came. A burly black man with a thick beard approached me and stuck out his hand.

"Hi, my name is Dennis, let me show you to your room so you can unpack.", giving my hand a firm squeeze. He walked me up the stairs and down a corridor with rooms on both sides. We approached what was to be my room and he pointed to the empty bunk among the others. "There you go, the top bunk is yours. Get unpacked and I will see you later."

I looked around at my new digs and felt the taste of vomit coming to the back of my throat. How did I wind up here? Was this the end of my quest for family? A fucking orphanage full of outcasts just like me?

"*Hey man, whatchu doin in here?*", a deep voice called out from behind me. I turned around to find a tall, muscular black kid with a bandanna on his head staring at me with an angry look on his face.

He was standing there with his arms crossed. There was a thick gold chain with a dollar sign charm dangling from his wide, sweaty neck. "*YO, you hear me? Whatchu think you doin in here boy?*", his eyes squinting, "*Who told ya you could be in dis room?*"

"Mr. Dennis brought me up here to unpack.", I responded as I looked down at his unlaced Adidas sneakers, tongues hanging out like a dog's in the summer heat. "I'm new here." I held out my hand, "My name is Steve.", he declined to accept my offer.

"Well, lissen here little man, don't touch nothin in here.", he rolled his eyes at me and turned around to walk down the hall.

I wanted to grab him and ask what this place was, but I was scared. Part of me knew, but the other part of me, the part that was unsure , really didn't want to know. I continued to unpack and when I finished, I went back downstairs to try to figure out what was supposed to happen next. I went out to the parking lot and found a spot in the shade to watch the kids play ball. There was trash scattered about the lot and the group of kids seemed to be blind to the fact that I was watching them. They just continued on with their game. Occasionally stopping to push each other with shouts of 'Foul', and 'No way man, you was out!' Shoving each other until they decided to resume play.

I just stared in amazement at this place that I was now stuck in. The other kids varied in age. Some looked to be as young as seven or eight, while others could have been grown men for all I knew.

No one really talked to me on the first day. Instead, they stood clear and observed. They were probably trying to get a read on the type of person I was. Maybe to determine if they could get something out of me. I had nothing for them, and they seemed to know it. I spent the next two days in my own solitude amongst the other orphans.

On the third day at Kilbarchen, the staff took us to a football charity football game. There were members of the New York Giants who were playing some of the local business owners. The game was held at a field in Union, New Jersey, just two miles from Hillside, where I grew up. I decided to use this as a chance to get away from this place.

When the rest of the bunch and staff were deeply into watching the game, I slipped away from the bleachers and out of the park. I ran and ran until I couldn't even see the park behind me. Cutting from street to street, I made my way to my Nanny's house. Out of breath from my running, I sat down on the back staircase for a few minutes before heading upstairs to her apartment. There was no answer when I knocked, so I decided to wait for her to come home from wherever she was.

Nanny came home a few hours later to find me sitting on her doorstep. We hadn't seen each other since before the whole Nikki fiasco, so she was, to say the least, shocked to see me.

"Steven, what are you doing here?", her voice squeaky, "How did you get here?", she continued.

"Nanny, I ran away from the place that they put me in. It was an orphanage Nanny.", I had tears in my eyes , and there was a lump in the back of my throat. It felt like there was someone trying to choke me from the inside out.

Nanny cried out, "An orphanage? What do mean an orphanage?", as she opened the door and shuffled me inside, "I thought that you were in a foster home?", obviously confused by all of this.

"I was, but that was a while ago. Last week, I was sent to an orphanage.", I sat down at the kitchen table while she put the kettle on the stove for tea, "Please don't make me go back there.", looking at her with the eyes of a saint.

I went on to tell her everything that had happened in the past year. She watched in amazement as I spilled my guts. I could tell that she really didn't know too much about where I had been, or what I was going through. She told me that the last she heard, I was in a foster home.

Nanny agreed that I shouldn't go back to Kilbarchen, and called my father to fill him in about the recent events going on in my world. After a discussion between them from which I could only gather bits and pieces, "No Robert, you listen to me…No…You need to step up…OK…see you then…", she hung up the phone and looked at me sitting there waiting for an explanation.

"I am going to drive you down to your father's", her tone comforting but serious, "But you MUST behave.", I was nodding in disbelief that she had worked it out, "Steven, do you hear me? You MUST behave yourself. Your father won't tolerate any nonsense."

I acknowledged her statements, and we left the house for the drive down to Neptune. I didn't want to see Nikki, but I was glad that dad was convinced to take me back. If only Nanny would have stepped in last year. Maybe then I wouldn't have had to endure all of the shit that I had been through.

DAD & NIKKI'S APARTMENT: NEPTUNE, NEW JERSEY
JULY 17, 1987

He had a very serious look on his face as Nanny walked me through the front door. I was almost ashamed to look at him. Nikki was sitting on the velvet couch with her eyes looking right at me, cutting through me to my very soul. I took a deep breath and stepped into the foyer. Looking up at my father for the first time in a year, I couldn't find a word to speak. I didn't have to. Nanny sensed the tone in the air and walked the two of us into the kitchen. Pointing at Nikki, she said,

"You stay there! We…", pointing at my father and I, "…need to have a talk!"

She had one of her tiny hands around my arm and the other around her son's. Leading us like we were a pair of scolded children. Which, given the nature of the situation, we actually were. We were her children.

She sat both of us down like the children that we were, and made us sit and talk in front of her until she was comfortable enough with our rapport to leave us alone. As we sat there, Nanny went into the living room to speak with Nikki. A few minutes later she came back and said that she was leaving.

Dad and I walked her to the door and she gave me a hug and kiss goodbye. She looked at dad and patted his chest and said, "Make sure you do the right thing Son."

As he closed the door behind her, Dad's look completely changed. He grabbed my arm very harshly. Dragging me into the living room, he shoved me down on the couch and fiercely spoke at me, waving his arms in the air like a madman.

"I don't know what your Nanny may have told you, but this was NOT my idea", looking over at Nikki he continued, "We are not really thrilled to have you here.", he stopped to take a deep breath, "If you are going to be here you WILL obey the rules of this house.", his voice getting louder as he spoke, "You WILL do whatever either of us tell you to. Do you understand me?"

"Yes.", I nodded in fear, "I understand." Although I really didn't understand, nor did I agree.

"Tell her…", shifting his eyes towards Nikki, "that you understand." He stood there firmly with his hands across his chest.

I looked over at Nikki and spoke, "I understand!", my tone non committal, and my body language apathetic.

"Now I want you to apologize for what you did to her.", his eyes said that he was very serious.

I sat there in defiance. Why should I apologize? Hadn't I paid enough? Shouldn't they be apologizing to me? Wasn't it them who had thrown me away like I was a rag doll? Dad didn't take my defiant stare well. He picked me up and threw me across the living room.

"I told you to apologize dammit!", he grabbed me up and dragged me to the bedroom, "Now, you stay in here and you don't come out.", He slammed the door and walked off.

It seemed to me that I was in the same boat that I was in just a year ago. I was back to being forced into a room. Dad was yelling and screaming again. He had hit me again. It occurred to me that in the morning he might drag me back to the DYFS office and drop me off again. They would probably take me back to Kilbarchen, or maybe someplace worse. I couldn't let that happen again. I wanted to be dead. It had to be better than the life that I was living. After seeing all of the shit that I had seen, I realized that death was the only answer to my problems. Death was my way out. I would embrace death and if there was a God, then soon enough I would be able to ask him face to face just why he picked me to be his rag doll.

I had to die. I wanted it! Needed it! I went into the bathroom undetected and opened the medicine cabinet. On the top shelf there was an orange bottle of prescription pills with a label that read: Darvon. I read the label and determined that this would take care of my problem. The bottle was nearly full. I grabbed a cup of water and started to take handfuls of the pills until they were gone. Following each mouthful with a huge gulp of water. I plopped down on the floor next to the toilet and waited for death to embrace me. I welcomed its cold grip. The next thing I remember is my dad shaking me awake.

"Steven, wake up.", shaking me hard, "I'm gonna get you some help,..NIKKI CALL AN AMBULANCE!!",

That was the last thing I remembered. Everything else is blank. I woke up in a room at Jersey Shore Medical Center sometime in the middle of the night. Dad was sitting there right beside me.

"Why?", was all that he could say. His eyes red from crying at the near loss of his first born Son., "Why?"

"I don't know Dad, I thought you hated me.", I responded with shame for my seemingly selfish deed.

"I don't hate you Son, I just don't understand you.", he leaned forward, whispering, "I am the one who should be sorry Son."

"What is going to happen next Dad?", I was scared that he was going to leave me there, "Are you gonna send me away again?", I could see from the look in his eyes that he was. If he was going to send me away again, why didn't he just let me die there in the bathroom. Why subject me to more pain and suffering?

"It's not up to me now Steven. The doctors are going to take you somewhere to make sure you don't do this again and when you are better, you can come home.", I could see that he really didn't want to let them take me away. He didn't have a choice. "I will come and see you every weekend Son, I promise. I will help you get through this."

A Doctor came in and cleared his throat. He nodded his head toward my dad and then toward me, and spoke,

"It's time for your Son to go." Dad stood up and gave me a hug. The male nurse walked in and strapped my arms to the side of the bed. I was scared, but I figured that I would be going back to Piscataway. Dad followed us all the way to the ambulance. Before they closed the door, he said to me,

"You will be ok. I love you and I will see you soon."

"I love you too Dad!", and with that the door was shut and the ambulance was rolling down the road. Still tired from the effects of the pills still remaining in my system after my stomach was pumped, I fell asleep before we even got out of the parking lot.

ARTHUR BRISBANE
CHILD TREATMENT CENTER:
ALLAIRE, NEW JERSEY
JULY 1987

I slept for almost thirteen hours. I woke up groggy eyed in a strange place with a strange man hovering over me.

"Where am I?", looking at the man with tired eyes, "Who are you?", confused by drug induced slumber.

"You are at Brisbane. My name is Chris Hill.", he stuck his hand out toward mine, "I am here to watch over you."

"I shook his hand, "Um..Chris, what is this place?"

"It's a treatment center for kids who have emotional problems. Do you know why you're here?", he asked. I thought for a second. I had remembered the pills, and the ambulance, but everything else was a blur. I shook my head for a second and looked at him.

"I tried to kill myself?", half answering, and half asking, "I took a bunch of pills."

"Yeah, they brought you in late last night. You have been sound asleep ever since.", raising his dark eyebrows.

"What time is it?", not sure just how long I had been sleeping.

Looking at his watch, he replied, "About five thirty. Are you hungry? You should probably eat something."

I nodded, " I have to use the bathroom.", as I stood up from the bed, unsure if my feet and legs were going to work as intended.

"Sure, come on, follow me.", he led me to an orange tiled bathroom with a long row of sinks and toilets. As I stood at the urinal to piss, I looked back over my shoulder at him standing there.

"I can take it from here, Thanks.", he just stood there and waited for me to go. "Really man, I got it from here."

"Sorry little dude.", he exclaimed, "I am your permanent shadow. Everywhere you go, I go too.", clearing his throat, "It's called a suicide watch. I gotta make sure you don't try to hurt yourself again."

I took a deep breath and tried to concentrate on the task at hand. After about a minute of deep concentration, I pissed as if it was my first time in years.

"Ok, let's get you something to eat. You must be hungry after that long nap.", Chris walked me down the stairs and outside. "I will give you a little tour of the campus."

As we were walking down the walkway, I looked around. This place looked like it was out in the middle of nowhere. Like a small school campus dropped in the middle of a forest. There was another identical building right to the one we just exited. A huge baseball field and a building on the other side of the field that Chris said was the school building. "Over there..", he pointed to a narrow walkway, "Just past the admin building is where the pool is."

We went into a large building that resembled an old colonial mansion. This was the administration building. We walked down the huge inner staircase into a modern cafeteria, where I got a tray full of food and ate. Chris went on to tell me while I was eating that this whole place used to be the private estate of a very wealthy man named Arthur Brisbane. Arthur had left his land to the state. Much of it, over 1200 acres, had been turned into Allaire State Park. Which explained why I thought I was in the forest. I was.

Over the next week, Chris and I would spend all of my waking hours together. After the first few days, I could tell he was getting tired of having to escort me and watch me everywhere I went. I had to eat separately from the other kids. I had to shower separately. I even had to sleep in a separate area. One day, as we were walking around the campus, I asked Chris if he could show me the pool.

"Sure dude, but you can't go in. Don't want you to try to drown yourself.", he said in jest as he led me down a driveway lined with garages on the right. "This is where Arthur kept all of his cars. He was a very rich man!", giving a little laugh, "I sure wish that I had a place like this of my own!"

A few days later, after speaking with a few of the staff doctors, I was finally released from my suicide watch. I began to integrate with the other kids. I was assigned a room to sleep in. I was given some tests to determine the level of my education, and subsequently assigned to a small classroom where I would go to school everyday. Little by little, I was granted privileges such as being able to watch TV, and playing pool. I eventually got to go swimming in the olympic sized pool that Mr. Brisbane had left for us.

My days were filled with school, and my evenings consisted of recreation. This place wasn't so bad. I really didn't have anything to do but behave. I got to call my mom whenever I wanted. I even called my dad. He told me that he wanted to come and see me. After arranging it through the staff, he came up the following weekend.

When he got there, I was told that we weren't allowed to leave the area beyond the baseball field. Once we had a successful 'On-Campus' visit, then we could arrange for day visits where dad could take me away from the center for the day. As we walked around the edge of the field, Dad lit a cigarette and handed it to me. I had picked up the habit in the in-patient unit, and dad didn't seem to mind.

"Here...", he said as he handed it to me, "You probably need one of these, huh?", I took a drag and exhaled slowly. The dizzy feeling came right to me. It had been nearly 3 weeks since I had smoked. Dad looked at me and asked if I was doing ok.

"I'm ok Dad, this place isn't so bad.", handing him the cigarette. He gave it back to me after using it to light another for himself. "Thanks.", I responded. This was going okay, I thought. Maybe things will be alright after all. Puffing away on the cigarette.

"So...Next time, what do you say we go and see a movie or something?", Dad asked as we were walking, "Or whatever you decide you want to do. Just you and me kid.!", the corner of his mouth turned up in a half grin.

I told him I would give it some thought. We spent the rest of the afternoon just roaming around the field. Talking like we hadn't done in a very long time. Just pointless conversation mainly, but it was nice to have that avenue open after so long.

He left and I looked forward to our next visit. Which was to be two weeks later. The following weekend, mom and my little brother Robert came up. Since it was raining out, and all of the other kids were on a field trip, we hung out in the rec room. Robert and I shot pool while mom just kind of lingered in the background. I could tell that she was uncomfortable being there. Although I wasn't sure if it was this place that was making her uncomfortable, or if it was me. It could have been a combination of both.

"So, I understand that your father came to see you. How did that go?", She asked me with a blank look on her face. Her voice was kind of monotone and noncommittal.

"It was ok Mom. He said that he would be back next week to take me out for the day.", I waited for her next move. It was clear that she saw me being here as partly his fault. I doubted that she would accept any of the blame. In her mind, there was no way that she could be culpable in any of this. I could tell that by her face. This was all HIS fault. Mom looked at me with concerned eyes,

"Steven, Why did you do it?", she asked with care. A slight gloss was covering her eyes.

"I don't know Mom. I guess that I just got fed up.", I looked over at Robert. He had no real idea what was going on. Stepping over to my mom, I spoke softly to avoid him hearing me, "I couldn't take it anymore, and....I just wanted it to be over, I guess."

She reached out her hands and hugged me close, "I'm sorry that you have had to go through all of this Son. I don't know what to do for you."

I broke from her embrace. Giving a look that said: You know you can do? You can take me home with you! Even though I didn't say a word. She knew right away from the look on my face just what I wanted. It was the same thing I had wanted for more than a year. I wanted a real home.

She just sighed, "I can't take you with me. I just don't think you are ready for that.", she paused, "I just don't think that WE'RE...", her eyes gestured toward Robert, "ready for that right now." Obviously she thought I was going to corrupt my little brother. It probably didn't enter her mind that I just wanted a family of my own again. It was then that I realized there was more to this than I was seeing. My own mother was scared of me. She was afraid that I would not only screw up her happy life, but more so that I would wind up screwing up my little brother's head. It was as if I was a demon and this place was the priest who was supposed to exorcise my evil spirit. I just gave her a blank stare. I couldn't even think of anything else to say to her. My silence was her hint to leave. She took it.

That was the way it went for a while. She would come up every few weekends and take me out. But never once was a word mentioned about me coming to live with her. Nor was anything else ever said about what had put me here. It was all smoke and mirrors. She took me shopping or to the movies and I let her. Using guilt as my vice, I made her pay for the mistakes that were made in the past. The weird thing was that the both of us seemed to be content with that.

Dad was a different story altogether. When he came to take me out, we would routinely speak on what had happened. He had no problem talking about my loose screws, or his own for that matter.

"Listen, I am aware that I am a bit messed up son.", he said one day as he was driving, "But you have got to understand that anything I ever did to you was done because I love you." I didn't believe a word that he said. I knew that abandoning a child, whether it was the California thing, or the foster care thing, was wrong. I knew that he was just as screwed up as I was. Most of the time though, I didn't care. I just relished his company. I had come to the conclusion that this is the person he was, and I was the person that I was. There was nothing, in my eyes, that either one of us could do about it. We were a pair of 'Fuck Ups'. He was a drunk. I was crazy. That was that. As long as I got to see him, I was alright. I had started to shift the blame for my problems from him to my mother. It became her fault for leaving me with him that I got screwed up.

Things continued like that for me for a few months. I would spend most of my weekends out with dad. My mother's visits became more rare. As time passed, I missed her less and less. Before I knew it, it was the middle of Fall and my time at Brisbane was coming to an end.

Yet another DYFS caseworker came to see me to explain the next course of action in my case. I would be going to a new residential program. A place that was more long-term. I really didn't care where they sent me anymore. I was growing accustomed to life away from home. I just shrugged my shoulders at him and said, "OK, Whatever." As long as I got to go out with my dad on weekends, I didn't care where I was going. I knew that this was going to be a way of life for me. I would be wherever they put me. I gave into the struggle. A new kind of monster was growing inside of me.

I was becoming an institutionalized child. It became all I knew. I had forgone the ways of a normal life for normal children and let the chips fall as they may. I was tired of fighting and screaming about not being able to have a real home. Those things no longer mattered to me. I was giving in to the system that had created me. If my past placements made me a little apathetic, the next one would turn me into a real monster. One who didn't care about the consequences of any of his actions. This next place wasn't just for kids with family or emotional problems. This next place, as it would turn out, was also for criminals. It would become my college and I would graduate with honors.

BURLINGTON COUNTY CHILDREN'S HOME: MOUNT HOLLY, NEW JERSEY NOVEMBER 1987

If Kilbarchen looked old, then this place was ancient. The Fall air was crisp as I stepped out of the standard state issued Dodge K-Car and looked around. There was an assortment of brick buildings strewn about like a tornado had dropped them there. The only thing which resembled a modern structure was off in the far left corner of a grassy field. The building's metal roof gave away that it was a gymnasium. "What? No swimming pool?", I said in a sarcastic tone to the new caseworker whose name I didn't even care to remember. He just grunted and walked me toward one of the brick buildings, where he left me without a word.

Looking around the office, I could spot old black and white photos on the walls of groups of children standing in front of the smaller building strewn about the campus. The kids in the photos were dressed in a manner that told me that this place had been around for a very long time.

"That one is from 1958.", a voice came from beside me, "That was taken in front of 'Riley Cottage'", I looked to see a man standing there pointing at the photo I was looking at. "Which is where you're going to be staying.", like all of the people I had met before, he stuck out his hand and gave me the usual greeting, "Hi, I'm Rich London, I will be your counselor.", he went on talking more, but the only thing I heard was "Blah, Blah, Blah, Ba-blah, Blah."

Rich walked me around pointing around to this building and that building. When we approached one on the far right side in the back of the grounds, I began to pay attention to his words again.

"This right here is Riley Cottage. This will be your new home.", as he walked me up the old brick stairs, cracked and abused by years of neglect. "We will get you situated before lunch.", guiding me inside.

I looked around as we walked in the building. There was a living room area off to the right. Sofas with large wooden frames and plaid cushions that resembled burlap sacks. The carpeting was a classic green shag that hadn't been cleaned in at least fifteen years. On the far side of the dingy shag was a television that screamed out a look that said HELP! It was a wooden floor model with the finish worn down to almost nothing. There weren't any buttons or knobs left on the front, just a ball point pen sticking out of the hold that used to house the power switch.

To the left of the little foyer, was a short hallway that led to two small rooms on the end. The room on the right had one wooden framed bed and dresser in it. The one on the left had the same, but there were two beds and dressers instead. I got the room on the left.

"There you go.", pointing at the empty bed, "That is going to be your bed right there.", Rich looked around for a second and found which dresser was empty, "You can put your clothes in here."

While I unpacked, he walked off to an office that I hadn't noticed when we walked in. I found him there on the phone when I finished. He held up a finger to tell me to hold on for a second.

"I'll be right with you.", he went back to the phone, "Uh-huh, I see..Ok.Goodbye.", walking out he said, "Are you all set?", When I nodded yes, "Good, now let's go and get you some chow." I followed him through the maze buildings to what they called the Chow Hall. When I walked in everybody inside stopped eating and looked at me with curious eyes. I was the new guy again. The other kids pointed and nodded to each other. Whispering things among themselves. Most of them seemed older than me by at least four or five years. I tried to ignore their stares. I got a tray containing the day's mystery meat and potatoes and sat down at the first open seat I could find.

"That seat is taken bro.", a blond haired kid proclaimed. He tried to stare at me with menacing eyes. I just ignored his stares and started to eat. "Yo, I SAID that seat is taken, didn't you hear me?", I just looked at him with raised eyebrows and continued to chew my food.

He stood up to try and make a scene. Apparently he assumed that him standing up was supposed to intimidate me, but it merely set me off. I just grabbed my tray and tried to bury it in the side of his face. I must have hit him a good six or seven times before I heard the plastic tray crack. He obviously didn't want a problem, because he didn't do anything but try to cover his head. I took his maneuvers lightly and started to punch him. I don't know how many times I actually hit him before the staff members pulled me off. I couldn't see anything but him. In my mind, the room was empty. I was completely oblivious to anything or anyone else but the two of us. Once I was pulled away, the rest of the room came into view. I saw that the other kids were just staring in disbelief at what had happened. They were used to seeing fights, as I later found out. But it was a rare occurrence for one to start in the chow hall, especially by a new kid. I was dragged out of the chow hall and taken back to the office that I had just been dropped off in just an hour before. Rich had followed me through the door and told me to calm down.

"What the hell was that about?", he asked as I sat there breathing heavily.

"He stood up and tried to start with me.", I answered between breaths. Truth be told, I knew what I was doing. I was trying to make an impression on the other kids.

"Son, you don't start a fight just because someone stands up to you, and you sure as shit don't beat someone in the head with a tray!", he just stared at me like he had never seen such an act.

"Listen man, the way I was brought up, someone steps to you , you deal with it.", although that really wasn't the case. Dad had told me to never start a fight, but I no longer put much faith in the things that he told me.

"Go back to the cottage. I will deal with you later!", Rich belted out in frustration. I had made an impression alright. Not just on the kids, but on the staff too. I wondered what my punishment would be for my first day's actions. What could they really do to me? Call the police? Not very likely. I just strolled back to the cottage with my head held high.

"Yo man, where you from?", a lanky black kid asked me as I plopped on the ratty sofa.

"All over.", I really didn't have a hometown anymore, so that wasn't a hard question to answer, "I grew up living up north in Hillside and Bayonne."

"Yeah, I thought that was some North Jersey shit that you did.", he slapped my hand, "I'm George, but they call me Gee. I'm from Newark. What's your name, little bro?"

"I'm Steve, and they call me Steve!", I slapped his hand back and we both laughed.

"I like you little man! Alright!", he grabbed me on the arm, "Come on, I'll introduce you to some of the fellas.", he led me out into the back of the cottage where some of the kids were just hanging out and smoking.

When the other kids saw Gee walking me around the back, they all stopped what they were doing and looked at us with their full attention. We stopped and he put his hand on my shoulder, "YO, everyone, this here is Steve from 'Up North', his eyes darting around the bunch, "Steve, this is the fellas!"

He walked me around them, introducing me one by one. There was Little Man from Patterson, Joker from Elizabeth, Larue from Jersey City, and Sha from Newark. Just like Gee, all of them were black. There were no white kids in this bunch. They all just shook or slapped my hand and made comments like, 'What up', or 'Hey Bro'. I was taken in by this bunch of guys. Wherever they went, I went. We all stood together for anything we did.

There was no real punishment for my actions in the Chow Hall that first day. I just had to stay 'On Grounds' for three days. Which was fine with me, because I didn't have anywhere else to go. Some of the 'fellas' went out that night and brought me back some smokes and some junk food. Which was good, because I didn't have any money. They looked out for me like I was one of their little brothers.

A few days later, as we were all walking to the school building for our daily classes, the kid that I beat up in the Chow Hall approached us.

"Listen here man, you mess with Steve, you messing with all of us!", Gee said to him as he put himself between us.

"I don't want to start anything. I just wanted to apologize for what happened the other day.", he held out his hand to me, "Look man, I didn't mean anything by it. I was just messing around.", I looked around for a second at everyone else and dropped my shoulders in an awkward manner.

"All right, It's cool.", I shook his hand and walked off. The rest of the guys followed as I walked with my head held high and my shoulders back.

"Yo man, why you shake his hand?", Larue said as we walked in the door to the school building.

I turned around and gave him a devious grin, "Never know when I might need him for something!", was the only response I offered. Everyone but Gee and Sha looked confused by my answer. Apparently they both got the gist of what I was getting at.

"Yeah man, Check it out, he's right.", Gee replied. He could see that I knew how to anticipate future dealings with people. "There may be a day where we need little blondie over there to take care of something for us. Steve just kept the channels open for that. Plus now the kid knows that whatever we need from him, we are gonna get because instead of getting his ass kicked again by Steve, he would have to deal with all of us!", making them understand better.

Only about a quarter of the kids at Burlington were there because of their emotional or family problems. The rest, my new friends among them, were criminals. Drug dealers, car thieves, violent offenders. They were all city kids. Mostly growing up in the ghettos of Newark, Patterson, Jersey City or Elizabeth. These were the kids who took me under their wing and schooled me on the points of life that I didn't know about. I would spend hours and hours under their tutelage. I listened to their stories of stolen car chases, or how to cook crack cocaine to get the most profit. I sat in awe as they broke down their trades. The same way a normal child my age would stare at the TV in awe of some cartoon that he loved. But I was not a normal child anymore. Any resemblance to normalcy had long since been dissolved. I was becoming something else, something worse.

Life went by for me at Burlington in a rather easy fashion. Dad started coming down on the weekends and would take me out for the entire day. As Christmas was approaching, he asked me if I wanted to go and spend some time at Nanny's house during the holidays. All of the kids who had somewhere to go could leave for the entire holiday season if they wanted. I was happy to be able to go and spend some time with her. He told me that even though I couldn't come and stay with him for Christmas, he would drive up to Nanny's and come see me.

The weekend before my twelfth birthday, mom and David came down to see me. They took me out and bought me a new boom box and some new clothes to celebrate my special day. I decided to see what their plans were for the holidays.

"Mom, what are you guys doing for Christmas?", I knew that she really didn't want me to come and stay with her, but I asked anyway, "Can I come and visit for a few days?"

She tried dodging my question, "What is your father doing?", I didn't answer her.

I already had my plans to go to Nanny's, but mom didn't know that. "Steven, it's just not a good time right now. I'm sorry, but I don't think it would be right for you to come up to our house.", she said as David steered the car back to Burlington.

"That's alright, I think I am just going to go up to Nanny's house for a while.", trying my best to make her jealous. I knew her distaste from my other Grandmother. My ploy to rile her up didn't work though. Instead, she just replied,

"It would be good for you to spend some time with your Nanny. Especially since she lives by herself."

That was the end of it. When we got back, it was like the conversation never took place. I didn't know it at the time, but that would be the last time I would see my mother and David for nearly four years.

I took a train to Linden, which was where my Nanny was now living. Linden was only about a ten minute drive from Hillside where she used to live. Christmas was rather quiet considering it was just the two of us. Dad had broken his promise to come and visit me while I was there, and I wasn't surprised. He probably figured that I would pester him about coming to live with him again. Either that, or Nikki forbade him from coming. In my mind, with one was likely.

About two days after Christmas, I felt very anxious to get back down to Burlington. I didn't want to be stuck here in the house with my aging Nanny. I wasn't due back until the third of January, but I decided that I should go back anyway. When I told Nanny, she was confused.

"What do you mean you want to go back? Is someone going to be there to watch you if you go back early?", she asked as I started to gather my things.

"Yes Nanny, there are still kids who didn't go home for Christmas.", trying to make her realize that I was no longer in a foster care setting.

"Well, how will they know you are coming back? You should call them and let them know that you are coming.", she said with concern.

"I will call them from the train station when I get down there. Now can you please take me to catch the train?", looking at my schedule, "The next one leaves in twenty five minutes.", I continued in an irritated voice. She just gave in and frantically began to look for her purse and car keys so she could take me.

"Okay, I will drive you. But I want you to call me when you get there.", she said as we were walking out the front door, "I am too old to be sitting up all night worrying about you."

Nanny dropped me off, and two hours later I was arriving in Burlington. I made a call to my cottage and they said they would come and pick me up.

As 1988 rang in, I spent New Year's Eve getting high on the roof of the cottage with two of the other kids who weren't able to go home for the holidays. Instead of letting the world bring them down, they decided to walk into town to get a bag of weed. I was more than happy to join them in their celebration.

For me, the next few months brought more weekend visits from dad. More drugs to use and more trouble to get into. There was constant fighting between the kids of North and South Jersey, as well as between cottages. With my new crew being the main instigators. Often, we would single out a group of kids from another cottage who hailed from the South and start with them. The two groups would fight until there was enough blood spilled between us to be satisfied.

Oddly, the staff never really interfered in our little outbursts. They would just sit back with the 'Kids will be kids' attitude and let us kick the shit out of each other until our hearts were content. The only real thing that the staff in Burlington did was make sure we got fed, went to our classes and got in and out of bed on time. Otherwise, they really weren't all that visible. They would sit in the office and keep their distance.

It's amazing that they really had no idea about some of the things that went on there on a regular basis. From drug use, to rampant sexual experimentation activity, to even rape. Either they didn't know or they didn't care. Things like rape didn't occur everyday, but it did occasionally happen. There were a lot of kids who were bigger and stronger than others, and sometimes those kids would prey on the weaker ones. Some of the things that I saw throughout my time there, I would love to forget.

The staff sometimes took us roller skating on Saturday nights, and the majority of us guys would use that time to hook up with local girls. We'd skate with them, and make out with them until it was time for us to go. The girls all knew we were in a home. I think that it just made us all the more interesting to them. There were a few that lived only a few blocks from our campus, and once I made the necessary arrangements with them, I would walk away from Burlington for days at a time. I would spend those days like I was a free man. Hanging out with the girls, having them sneak me into their bedrooms at night. Just a twelve year old boy trying to make his mark in the world.

I really didn't care about getting into trouble for my little trysts. Similar to being AWOL in the Army, only the staff would just write it down in a log book that you were gone. When you came back or were brought back by the police, you would lose some of your privileges for a few days. No big deal.

It was in the midst of serving one of my little sentences for walking off, that dad showed up unexpectedly. I was walking toward the chow hall when I saw a familiar car pulling into the parking lot. I broke away from the group of kids that I was walking with and ran toward the car.

"Dad, Hey!", I exclaimed, as I gave him a hug. "What are you doing here?"

He gripped me in his arms, "Hey little man, I came down to see you!", When he let go, I could see from the look on his face that something was different about him. He looked changed. "Hey, let's take a ride, huh?", as he looked around for someone to ask permission from.

"Don't worry about them Dad, we can go.", I knew that there really was nothing that could be done to me if I left with my dad. I am sure that one of the kids told someone that it was my dad that I was running off to see. They all knew who he was from the weekends when he would come and pick me up.

I jumped in the car, and as we were driving down Route 38, I was starting to wonder why he just showed up in the middle of the week. What was this sudden urgency to see me? Had something happened to Nanny? Was there something wrong with him? He pulled into a diner parking lot and we went inside for a bit to eat.

"Listen Steven, I have something important to talk to you about.", he said as he sipped his coffee.

"What's up Dad?", I asked with curiosity.

"I have been doing a lot of thinking. I want you to come home.", he paused to light a smoke, "The problem is that I spoke with Nikki about it and she doesn't want you there."

That was it. The usual let down. As my face turned downward into a frown, he continued.

"That is why I am leaving her Son.", he looked me right in the eye and I wondered if I had heard him right.

"Did you say that you were leaving her?", my tone confused and my head spinning, I tried to process what he had just said.

"Yes, and in two weeks, I am coming to take you out of here and we are moving to Pennsylvania.", he answered with a growing grin.

"Oh my God Dad, that is the best news I have heard all year!", I reached down and grabbed one of his cigarettes and lit it. "Two weeks, really??"

"Really!", he responded with a smile, "I am going to call the people at DYFS and Burlington to let them know that you will be leaving. So, all you have to do is just sit back and wait."

There it was. My salvation from this life which was forced upon me! This stage was finally coming to an end. True to his word for once, dad came and signed me out of Burlington two weeks later. We spent about a week staying at a hotel during the transition of waiting for our new apartment in Allentown, Pennsylvania to be ready.

"Here's to our new life", Dad toasted me over our first dinner in our new apartment.

"A new state for our brand new life!", I toasted him back with a smile.

I had been torn from the trenches of a world that really didn't care about me, and thrown back into a world that would never understand me.

WHITEHALL APARTMENTS: ALLENTOWN, PENNSYLVANIA AUGUST 1988

Our new apartment was right on the edge of Route 22, directly across the highway from the Lehigh Valley Mall. There was a swimming pool for the residents to use and we had our own third floor balcony overlooking the highway. Compared to my surroundings over the past few years, this place was like a sanctuary for me.

Dad was working as a sales rep for a pest control company in Clinton, New Jersey. Clinton was just about a twenty five minute drive from Allentown. He had discovered that it would be cheaper to live in Pennsylvania and commute to Jersey for work. I wasn't thrilled about living in another state, but I went along with it. At least in the beginning. I was still trying to adjust to living in a normal everyday home. I had grown so accustomed to not being 'at home', that I really didn't know how to react to simple things like being able to open the refrigerator to get something to eat whenever I wanted. It was weird for me to have this sudden burst of freedom.

The first week in my new home, I only left the house sporadically. I went swimming a few times, but most of my days were spent just sitting around the apartment. I would sit on the balcony for hours just watching cars go by on the highway below. The same way a kid would become homesick while away at Summer Camp, I was becoming homesick for the institutional life that I had been living.

This new world was almost too much to bear. It no longer made sense to me. I wasn't able to interact with the local kids. I had lost the basic social skills that a normal child had. Dad was too wrapped up in his own world to notice my affliction. He would go off to work in the morning, and come home to sit back in front of the TV with a beer. The old bond that we shared when I was younger was now gone. We barely spoke. Had I forced him to change his life? Was it me that was making him miserable in his own way? I couldn't bear to ask him any of this. I was too afraid of what his response would be.

Suddenly one day, I just wanted to get out of there. I wanted to run away. I figured that I could handle the world on my own. I would wait until the time was right, and I would leave this new prison. I would run away and start my own life. I would create my own society with the kids who were just like me. The wayward children of the world and I could create my own world. A world where we only depended on each other. Not on the adults who had disappointed us time and time again.

I formulated a plan in my head. I needed to get back to Burlington to get the members of my new society. I was a two and a half hour drive away though. I needed a way to get there. All at once, it came to me. Dad was asleep in his bedroom in a drunken slumber. The keys to his new company car were sitting in the kitchen, right next to his wallet. That would be my escape. The 1988 Ford Tempo sitting in the parking lot. I would have my own car. With a car to get away, I could get so far that there would be no way that anyone could find me.

I grabbed the keys and the wallet and crept toward the front door. I left dad a note saying that I was going to the mall and would be back later. It was about five thirty in the evening. I figured that I could get far enough away before he woke up. As long as he didn't need to go somewhere, I would get even further before he realized that the car was gone. I already knew how to drive. Dad had taught me years before, and my education at Burlington had given me more insight on it. The only problem for me was that I wasn't exactly sure how to get back there. I knew that Route 22 was the same highway that ran through my old hometown of Hillside, and that from there I could take the Parkway South. I would figure out the rest as I went. I started the car and slowly crept out of the parking lot. Getting on Route 22, I headed East.

Although I knew how to drive, it was scary to do it in traffic. I had a rough time dealing with the cars that were on both sides of me on the highway. After the first twenty minutes or so, I was fine. I continued East until I started to recognize where I was. The Parkway was around here somewhere. I wanted to pull over to ask where but was scared that someone would realize that I was way too young to be driving a car. Instead, I just kept on driving until I saw a sign that said 'Garden State Parkway' with an arrow pointing right.

I followed the signs and was heading South toward my supposed freedom. Now my greatest concern was that a passing motorist or worse, a State Trooper would drive alongside me and really notice that there was a kid driving this car. Oddly, neither happened. I made my way South with ease. I circumvented the toll booths that had attendants and went through the exact change ones. Before I knew it, I was nearing Exit 91. This was the exit for my mom's house. I figured that I could navigate my way down back roads from there and got off at her exit.

As the sun was beginning to set, I drove right past mom's house. I was tempted to park the car and knock on her door, but I just kept going. What I thought would only be a two and a half hour drive, was now turning into almost four hours with all of my detours. I located the road that would take me into Mount Holly and continued South. As the clock on the radio was reading nine thirty, I was pulling into Burlington's parking lot. I pulled the car behind the Administration building and crept through the field toward the cottages. As usual, there were a few kids hanging out on one of the porches. They were very surprised to see me.

"Yo, Steve, what are you doing here?", some kid whose name I didn't remember asked.

"I came to get Gee and Larue.", walking past them around the side of the cottage to look through the side window to look out for staff, "Go inside and tell them to come out.", I whispered to avoid further detection. Ge and Larue came out about a minute later and were shocked to see me.

"What the fuck are you doing here man?", Gee asked in confusion.

"Come on guys, get your stuff. I'm getting you out of here. I got a car. Let's go!", I exclaimed in a hushed tone of voice. They looked very surprised at my last statement. They just stood there with their eyes wide and jaws dropped.

"Come on!", I repeated. I wanted to get out of here before someone realized what was going on.

The two of them didn't bother to go back inside. They just followed me across the grass to the car.

"Where did you get the ride?", Larue asked as I unlocked the door. "How did you get the keys for it?", Gee chimed in. He had both stolen and been in stolen cars before, but getting a stolen car with the keys was rare.

"It's my dad's company car. I just took it while he was sleeping.", I stated in a cool manner as I started the engine.

We headed down Pine Street toward Route 38. The car was getting low on gas, so I needed to fill it up before we headed off.

"Where are we gonna go?", Larue said from the back seat as we headed down the road.

"Yo, we can go to Newark and hide out with my older brother for a while.", Gee responded, "He can probably get us some money for the car.", I really hadn't considered just where we would actually go, but this sounded like a plan to me.

I drove down the road looking for a gas station while they made plans for us to get situated in our new life on the run.

"Do you know how to get to Newark from here?", Gee asked as we drove.

"Yeah, I was just up that way earlier.", I retorted, as I was searching the road for a gas station. "We can go the same way that I came down here, but first I gotta get some gas.

I spied a gas station up on the left and pulled in slowly. As the attendant came toward me , I shouted, "Fill it up Dude!", Gee and Larue were laughing in the back seat.

"Gas tank is on the other side of the car.", the man stated as he stood there in his greasy coveralls. Staring at the group of us like he knew we weren't supposed to be in this car.

I maneuvered the car around the pump and pulled in the correct way. He pumped the gas and cleaned the windshield. Which was covered in soot from my travels.

"That'll be fourteen seventy three.", he said when the pump stopped. I gave him a twenty. He looked at it and said, "I'll go and get your change.", as he was walking inside slowly.

As we were waiting, Gee leaned over to me, "Let's get out of here. Dude's gonna call the cops!", his voice showing panic.

"He ain't gonna call no cops man. He just went to get the change!", Larue offered from the back seat.

I lit a smoke and agreed, "Yeah man, chill out! Here he comes now.", the attendant came back to the car and gave me the change. We drove off and headed back down the road.

I was making a mental plan of our future when I saw the flashing lights in the rearview mirror. This guy really did call the cops. Scared, I continued on for about a mile without pulling over.

"Yo man, punch it!", Larue screamed from the back. I wasn't sure what to do. Did I keep going? Did I risk a high speed chase? As I was pondering all of this, Gee spoke up,

"Look man, it's over. Just pull over!"

I gave in and directed the car to the side of the road. This was the end of my journey. Soon, I thought, I would be back in some placement yearning to be free once again. I gave into it. My destiny was already written. I was going to jail this time. There was no escaping it.

MY FIRST RUN-IN WITH THE LAW: MOUNT LAUREL, NEW JERSEY AUGUST 1988

I stopped the car and waited for the cop to approach the driver's side door. As he walked up, he seemed very surprised that such a young kid was in the driver's seat.

"Son, get out of the car.", he calmly said as his partner walked along the other side.

I complied and got out. Without another word, he directed me to his squad car. As I sat in the car and waited to see what would happen next, a second squad car pulled up. Gee and Larue were put into the second car.

Now that we were separated, my best guess was that we would be interrogated in little rooms with bright spotlights. The same way I had seen on TV. No such thing happened though. I was taken to the police station and they were taken back to Burlington. I was seated in an office and asked the standard questions; Name, Address, etc....

By the time I had been pulled over, one of the staff at Burlington had realized that Gee and Larue were gone, and one of the other kids told them I had picked them up in a car. They had called the police as well.

The cops had been on the lookout for me when they got the call from the gas station attendant about three kids driving around in a white Ford Tempo.

The cop sitting at the desk asked me, "Son, why would you take your father's car and drive all the way down here?" He almost looked amused when he spoke. "Don't you realize that you could have been seriously hurt if you had an accident?"

I didn't know what to say. I just looked at him with my glassy eyes and asked softly, "Am I going to jail?", He snickered and looked at me with a smile.

"No, you're not going to jail. We spoke with your father, and he will be down tomorrow to come and get you.", He shifted in his seat, "But in the meantime, you have to go and stay at the shelter and wait."

I took solace in the fact that I wasn't going to jail. I was concerned though. I figured that my dad wasn't thrilled about me taking his car. It had actually surprised me to hear that he would be along to collect me the next day.

WAITING FOR THE ABSENT FATHER: BURLINGTON COUNTY SHELTER AUGUST 1988

I was taken to the shelter at about three thirty in the morning. I was assigned a bed to sleep in until the next morning, when it was thought my dad would be there to collect me.

When I woke up, it took me a second to remember where I was. I got up and walked around for a few minutes trying to get my bearings. I looked around a little and spotted a staff member motioning me over to her.

"Come on in my office and have a seat.", she said as I approached her. I shrugged my shoulders and followed her softly spoken request. I figured she would explain more of the same that the cop had last night in the police station. Dad would be here to get me and so on. I sat down and she looked at me.

"Steven? Is it?", I nodded, "Well Steven, my name is Mrs. Walters and I am one of the counselors here.", she gave me a grin, "I spoke with your father a few minutes ago, and there is a slight problem."

"What's the problem?", I asked, curious to hear more.

"Well, apparently he is coming down this way to get his car in a few hours, but…", she paused and continued, "he stated on the phone that he wouldn't be coming to pick you up too."

"What do you mean he's not coming to get me?", I asked confused by the whole thing.

"He told me that he just wasn't going to take you. Just his car.", she took a breath, "He said that WE could deal with you and that it was no longer his problem.

"Can he do that?", I questioned, "Can he just leave me here without getting someone's approval?", I could understand why he didn't want to come and get me, but I still didn't expect him to leave me.

"Actually, he can't just leave you. I explained that to him on the telephone, but he just hung up.", She went on further to say, ``We are going to be taking you in front of a judge to determine what should happen next."

"Why a judge??", I asked

"Well, because your dad lives out of state, we need to have a judge decide what will happen next.", she explained.

A few days later I was taken to the County Courthouse to see a judge who would determine my fate. As I sat in the courtroom, it occurred to me that they may just send me back to Burlington. Seeing as I just left there just a few weeks prior.

When my name was called, I approached the bench with Mrs. Walters. I had never been in a courtroom before. So I wasn't sure what would happen next. When the judge was filled in on the current situation by Mrs. Walters. He looked at her curiously.

"Let me get this straight. His father came down here to collect the car, but decided to leave the child?", he seemed confused.

Mrs. Walters chimed in, "Yes Your Honor, he told me on the telephone that he wouldn't be coming to get his son.", she put her hand on my shoulder.

The aging judge looked down at us from this high bench, "...And the father lives in Pennsylvania. Is this correct?"

Mrs. Walters answered yes as I nodded along, "Yes, apparently they just moved there a few weeks ago."

"Well then, this is not OUR problem.", he looked at the both of us very seriously. I tried to give my best innocent face. He went on, "This is Pennsylvania's concern.", If the father is his legal guardian, and he doesn't live in New Jersey, I say we send the child back to him."

Mrs. Walters nodded her head along with him as he was talking. When he was finished she asked, "Do you think that we should contact the authorities in Pennsylvania to come and get him?"

He just started to shake his head, "No, No, No!", he exclaimed. "I say we put him on a bus back home.", he looked down at me,

"Son, do you want to go back to your father's house?", I nodded yes, "and do you know how to get there from the bus station?", he continued.

"Yes sir, I do.", I really wasn't sure how to get home from the bus station, but I figured that I could find my way if I needed to.

"Well, It's settled then. Take him to the Philadelphia bus terminal and put him on a bus back to Allentown!", with that, he slammed a gavel and we left the courtroom.

As scared as I was to deal with my dad, I was relieved to be getting on that bus. They gave me ten dollars to get something to eat, and to use for cab fare once I arrived back in Allentown. They waited until I got on the bus and it pulled away from the station before the drive off in a separate direction.

I spent the next two hours on the bus thinking about what dad was going to do to me when I walked in the front door. I wondered if he would be expecting me? I also thought about the ass kicking I would surely be getting.

Instead of calling a cab when I got into town. I decided to walk home. I needed to figure out how to approach my dad. I decided to call him and let him know that I was only a few blocks away.

"What do you mean you're just a few blocks away? How did you get here?", he said in an aggravated tone.

"The judge told them to put me on a bus home. So they did dad.", I explained, "I don't have a key for the front door."

"Just ring the buzzer when you get here dammit!", with that, he hung up the phone.

I exhaled hard as I took in what he had just said. He was really pissed. Both at me for what I had done, and because of the fact that they had sent me back.

BACK AT WHITEHALL APARTMENTS: AUGUST 1988

I walked back to the apartment complex and rang the buzzer for our apartment. When the door opened, I took the elevator upstairs. When I knocked on the door, dad opened it and just stared at me. He stepped aside and let me in. When he closed it behind him, I spoke.

"Dad, I'm….", WHACK!, he smacked me as hard as he could across my face before I could say another word.

"What the fuck is wrong with you?", he screamed, "I give up my entire life for you, and this is how you repay me?", he smacked me again, "You steal my fucking car?", he continued screaming. "I try to help you and you go and do this? What is wrong with you?"

"Dad, I'm sorry.", I wasn't sure what else to say. Instead of just hitting me again, he just said.

"Go to your room! I don't even want to look at you. You make me sick.", he grumbled as he pointed down the hallway.

I sighed and walked down the hall to my room. I closed the door behind me and sat down on my bed. I reached over and turned on the radio.

Dad just burst through the door and yelled, "Oh no, You will NOT be in here relaxing! There will be NO radio. There will be NO television!", he grabbed both the radio and the small TV that I had.

"I want you to sit in this room and think about what the hell was going on in your head when you drove off in my car!", he yelled as he slammed the door.

I remained in my room until the next morning. There was no dinner. There was no bathroom. I just sat there in my bed until I fell asleep. I was awakened by dad bursting through the door in the morning.

"Get up and get dressed.", opening my blinds to let in the glaring sunlight, "We have an appointment to get to!"

I got up, changed my clothes and used the bathroom. When I came out, he asked, "You ready?"

"Where are we going Dad?", I was scared that he was putting me away again.

"You'll see, Come on!", the tone of his voice gave me no hint of what I should expect. We got in the car and when he started the engine, he looked over at me,

"I know what you're thinking! But, No, I am not taking you somewhere to leave you.", he started to drive, "But you DO have to go and talk to the police."

"Why do I have to see the police?", I asked him, "What if they lock me up?"

As we pulled up to a red light, he looked over at me and said, "They aren't going to lock you up. They are going to charge you though. You have to realize that this car does not belong to me. It belongs to my company, and they want me to file charges.", He drove on as I sat there, "It was either that or they were going to fire me! What would you do?"

I didn't know what to think. I was getting charged with stealing a car. What did this mean for me? Was I going to jail? Were they going to lock me up? What was going to happen? I needed to know. I looked at my dad and asked in a scared voice, "Dad, what if they DO lock me up?"

"Just relax, they won't!", he then let out a little chuckle, "I'm really surprised that you found your way all the way down to South Jersey by yourself. How did you do that?", he inquired.

"I don't know Dad. I guess I just have a good sense of direction like you.", I sneered.
He just started laughing. We both laughed for a good minute before he stopped all of a sudden.

"Listen, you know you did wrong, don't you?, asking me with a very serious look on his face, "Don't you?"

"Yes Dad.", I answered in fear.

"And you know that I have to punish you for what happened, Right?", he spoke with a small amount of concern.

"Yeah.", I responded.

"OK, I want to get this behind us.", he pulled into the police station parking lot, "Just promise me that you won't do anything stupid like that again."

"OK Dad, I promise.", almost relieved that he hadn't remained irate.

"Don't worry, I won't let them lock you up.", he put his arm around my shoulder as we walked inside.

After more than an hour of answering questions and filling out forms, I was released into my Dad's custody. A court hearing was set up for later in the month to determine what would become of the charges.

When we got home, Dad sat me down at the kitchen table and pulled up a chair across from me. Looking at me directly in the eyes and asked,

"All of this stuff over the past few years has been really hard on you, huh?", I nodded.

"Look, I know that you have been through a lot, and I know that we really haven't talked about it. But I just want to put the past in the past, OK?", he reached across the table and put his hand on mine.

"Sure Dad", I said, "Let's let the past stay in the past.", my mood relieved.

"OK.", Dad said, "But I still have to punish you. So this is what we're going to do. You are grounded until school starts next month. OK?", he gave me a serious look again, "OK?", I stared at him in amazement of what he had just said. Grounded, that's it?, I thought to myself. "That means you don't leave the house at all! Do you understand?"

"Yes Dad.", I answered him softly.

"OK! Now what do you want for lunch?, I just shrugged my shoulders. "How about some chicken salad.", he continued.

"Yeah Dad. Chicken salad sounds great.", I answered with a smile.

"Chicken salad it is!", he made us sandwiches and that seemed to be the end of the whole thing. About two weeks later, the two of us went to court. I was given probation for the whole car ordeal.

I stayed in the house until school started and I began to get used to living with my dad again.

THE INEVITABLE SCREW-UP: ALLENTOWN, PA NOVEMBER 1988

I started the eighth grade at Whitehall Middle School and began to make new friends around the area. Things were going just fine for a few months. But like everything else in the past. I screwed that up too. I got involved with some kids that I shouldn't have been around. We wound up stealing an ATM card and checks out of some guy's mailbox.

After about a month of shopping sprees on some strange man's dime, I got caught with a large wad of cash in school. The principal, of course, called my dad to explain what happened. Dad came to pick me up from school and took me home. He sat me in the kitchen while he went to search my bedroom for more money. He wound up finding some of the checks and more money.

Needless to say, he was pissed. He told me that he was going to call the police on me. Then he beat me unconscious. When I came to, he was in his bedroom laying down. So I decided to grab my stuff and leave. I was now on probation and I didn't want to wait around to see what would happen if he had indeed called the police.

I went to see some friends of mine, and we went for a joyride in one of their mother's cars. It didn't take long before we were pulled over driving around in Bethlehem, the next town over. No one was charged with anything. When our parents were called to come and get us, everyone but me was picked up. Dad had once again refused to come and get me.

I was taken to a local children's shelter. The next morning, my new probation officer, whom I had never met before, showed up to explain my current situation to me.

"Steven, I am Joe Richards.", he shook my hand, "I am from the Juvenile Probation Office. There are a few things that we need to talk about."

He went on to tell me that he'd spoken with my father and told me of his unwillingness to have me in the house. He briefly mentioned the whole check and money thing, saying that he was unsure of whether there would be any criminal charges pending.

"At this point, we are unsure of what the victim is going to do.", Joe explained, "So, in the meantime, you are going to stay here at the shelter."

"What about school?", I asked, "Do I still get to go to school?"

"Yes, the staff here will drive you to your bus stop in the morning and will pick you up when you call in the afternoon.", he answered, "But, you are to report directly back here until this whole thing is settled! OK?"

What could I say to him?, "OK, Joe. I will call them.", I answered him.

"I don't want to have to come looking for you.", he looked at me with menacing eyes, "This is the first and only chance you will get with me. Got it?"

"Yes sir!", I answered. I felt like I was spinning down a spiral of terror. What was going to happen when this man who's money we had stolen decided that he wanted us punished for our deed? It was then, right in front of my new probation officer, that I decided in my mind that I wouldn't stick around to find out.

I went to school as planned. I got on the bus that afternoon, but got off before it got to my stop. I went to see one of the kids who was in on the check scam. I told him what had happened and got some money from him to take off with.

I took a bus to Philadelphia and made my way to Mount Holly. I needed to confer with some of my boys at Burlington. I don't know why I kept running back to that place, but I did. When one of the staff saw me walking around the grounds with my boy Gee, she called the police.

I was taken to the local police station , where they called Pennsylvania to figure out what to do with me. Someone in the probation office told them to keep me there until they could get there the next morning. They would be there to collect me.

When the men showed up in their van with the barred windows, I knew I was screwed. They put handcuffs and shackles on me and transported me to a Juvenile Detention Center in Doylestown, Pennsylvania. I had never been handcuffed before, let alone shackled. So you can only imagine what was going through my mind as I was being escorted through the buzzing doors of the detention center.

BUCKS COUNTY JUVENILE DETENTION CENTER: DOYLESTOWN, PA NOVEMBER 1988

Bucks County was the county directly below Lehigh County where I lived. Lehigh's detention center was closed, so Bucks was taking their cases. I didn't know what to expect from this new type of place. I was being locked up. I was strip searched for the first time in my life. I was locked in a cell. I was scared of what was to come next.

The next morning, I was once again cuffed and shackled and transported in a Sheriff's car to the Lehigh County Courthouse. The sheriffs put me into a locked cage they called a bullpen to await my court hearing. Joe Richards came down to see me, and as he stood at the gate of the bullpen, he only had a few words to say to me,

"Well, you screwed up and blew it.", he said, "Now it's time to pay the piper.", he walked off without another word.

The judge had decided it was necessary to keep me locked up until the best course of action was determined. I spent the next few months in the detentions center going back and forth to court. My thirteenth birthday came and went without any celebration or acknowledgement. I saw my dad in court a few days after my birthday and I spoke to him for the first time in nearly two months.

"Dad, I turned thirteen the other day!", I said to him outside of the courtroom. I was trying to initiate some sort of conversation with him.

He just looked at me with a defeated stare. "To tell you the truth Steven, I don't care. Frankly, I'm surprised that you have made it to thirteen."

That would be the last face to face conversation that I would ever have with him.

In the second week of January 1989, the judge decided that I would be sent to a diagnostic center to determine the best type of placement for me. Two sheriffs picked me up, and as usual, handcuffed and shackled me for the ride to Western Pennsylvania.

ADELPHOI VILLAGE DIAGNOSTIC CENTER: APOLLO, PA JANUARY 1989

Adelphoi Village consisted of an assortment of group homes for troubled teens. They were scattered around in Southwestern Pennsylvania. The group home that I was sent to was named 'Miller Home'. It was a two story house with a few large bedrooms on the second floor. Each bedroom had a few sets of bunk beds. The first floor contained an office, a living room, a kitchen and a dining room. In the basement was a rec room with a pool table and an assortment of games to keep the kids busy during down times.

Unlike other places I had been to, this one was unusually clean. The staff were pleasant and the whole environment seemed to be comforting. I would spend the next two months going through an assortment of tests and interviews with psychologists and child specialists to try and figure out what type of placement would suit me best. Once again, I had given in to this system. Only this time, instead of acting as I had in the past, I tried to actually let them help me. I answered all of the questions they posed honestly. I attended my daily group meetings with the other kids. I interacted with everyone there in a respectful manner. I wanted to get all of my issues out in the open.

I would spend hours talking to staff and doctors about all of the stuff I had been through over the years. I was the youngest kid there, so the staff kind of looked out for me in a parental way. The other kids were all in their mid teens, so they adopted me as sort of a little brother. I was going through the program with ease. Within two months of my arrival there, it was determined that I would best be suited by a long term placement. Someplace in which I could grow into a productive teenager.

HARBORCREEK YOUTH SERVICES: HARBORCREEK, PA
MARCH 1989

Harborcreek was just outside of Erie, which was located in the Northwestern corner of Pennsylvania, just across Lake Erie from Canada.

It had been there for decades, but was surprisingly well kept over the years. There were three separate units for its residents. Each unit had its own floor in the main building. The 'Junior Unit' was on the first floor. The 'Intermediate Unit', and 'Senior Unit' were located on the second and third floor. Because of my age, I was assigned to the Junior Unit.

The Junior Unit had about thirty kids in it, ranging from ten to fourteen years old. There were three large dormitory rooms with single beds and lockers to hold our belongings. There were also two single rooms which shared a bathroom between them.

The dorms were assigned by levels of accomplishments within the unit. The levels were: Delta, Alpha, Beta and Super Beta. Delta being the lowest and reserved for troublemakers. The single rooms were for the Super Beta's. Since I was new, I started out in the Alpha Dorm.

My first day was uneventful. I was assigned a bed and given a tour of the place. I met the teachers that would be teaching me in the school building. I was also assigned a counselor who was there to assist me through my development. He was a short man with a thin goatee, and the build of a jock.

"My name is Dave Titley.", he shook my hand, "I will be your counselor while you are here.", he seemed pleasant enough, and the two of us sat down to talk about my life. I explained everything to him from my parents divorce all the way up until the present. He had a look of astonishment on his face by the time I was done.

"You're barely thirteen years old!", he stated, "Why is it that you have been through so much?", he asked

"I don't know Dave. I've had a rough life so far.", I answered him as openly as I could, "It's just been hell!"

"Well, don't worry.", he responded as he patted my shoulder, "We'll help you get your life together."

Shortly after my arrival at Harborcreek, I met a woman named Christine Dance. Like Dave, she was a counselor as well. If Dave was like a big brother to me, then Christine would become like a big sister. She was about twenty years old when I met her. She was working her way through college at the time. Immediately, when we first met, I was drawn to her. Although she had a reputation of being a hard ass in the Junior Unit, she seemed to take a liking to me, or maybe it was pity. She easily saw through all of my bullshit, and always challenged me to be myself, regardless of what other people thought or said. I think that was probably the best thing about her. She was always up front with me.

I got into a daily routine of going to school during the day, and relaxing at night. I would spend my evenings shooting hoops or playing video games in the rec room. Christine was usually there in the evenings, and we would play video games together. She often brought in her own games for us kids to play. There was one in particular that she was having a hard time completing. So us kids would play it for hours everyday until the task was closer and closer.

As Summer was approaching, the teachers in the school decided that I would be better suited by attending the local high school. Plans were made for me to start my Freshman year at Harborcreek High School. It was a very intriguing idea to me.

Since I was going to be attending public school. I was given an allotment of money to spend on new clothes. Christine volunteered to take me shopping for my new wardrobe. She helped me pick out new clothes and sneakers to ensure that I wouldn't have any trouble fitting in. We continued to grow closer during the summer. She would routinely take me to her apartment on her days off. We would hang out and play video games. Sometimes she'd bring one or two of the other kids, but it seemed to me that I was the focus of her efforts. She was quite aware of my family background, and even took me to meet her own family. Which was great for me, because they always made me feel wanted.

Once school started for me in the Fall, the only thing I did at Harborcreek was sleep. I got involved with as many extra-curricular activities at school as I could. I was trying to avoid spending my spare time there. I enjoyed spending it with normal kids a whole lot more. All of the local kids knew that I was in 'The Boys Home', as they put it, but none of them seemed to mind.

As time passed on, I began to progress through the level system at Harborcreek. Soon enough, I was a 'Beta'. With that came more freedom around the home. I could write my own ticket when it came to my activities. I was given a small allowance to spend. On Thursday nights the Betas were taking out shopping to buy whatever we could afford with our savings.

Things seemed okay enough for me. I was leading the 'Residential Life' that I'd grown accustomed to over the years. While at the same time leading somewhat of a 'Normal' life by going to public school. For me it was a fair balance of both worlds.

The Thanksgiving holiday was approaching and most of the other kids were making arrangements to go home with their families for the holiday. Since my dad was missing in action, and my mom was four hundred miles away in New Jersey, Christine opted to take me to her mother's house with her for Thanksgiving. She pulled me aside one day,

"Would you like to come to my mom's with me for Thanksgiving dinner?", she asked with a smile, "Mom wants you to come, and so do I!"

I hugged her and said, "Yeah, I'd love to come!", with a cheery voice. I was ecstatic at her offer.

"Ok, I will pick you up on Thursday morning, and we'll go to mom's together.", she hugged me back.

Christine picked me up as planned, and we spent the day doing all of the normal Thanksgiving stuff. We watched football with her brothers, we had dinner, and in the evening we all sat around eating dessert while having a chat about this or that. By the time the evening came to an end, I didn't want to go back to the boys home.

After my holiday break was over, I went back to my normal routine of school and such. Christine had stopped working at Harborcreek shortly after Thanksgiving to devote more time to school. She came to see me on my fourteenth birthday to wish me well. We also made arrangements for me to come and spend a few days with her and her family during Christmas. As usual, the majority of the other kids were going to their own homes for the holiday. But, I was more than happy to spend mine with Christine.

My mom sent a package for Christmas and my birthday. Inside were the black Air Jordan IV's and Chicago Bulls Starter jacket that I had written to her about. I called her up to thank her for the gifts. I hadn't spoken to her since she had taken me out for my birthday two years earlier. She seemed pleased to hear that I was doing well in my new placement.

I spent my Christmas holiday season with Christine and her family, as planned. It was a wonderful time for me. I felt so at home with them and was thankful for their love. Once again, I dreaded going back to Harborcreek.

In Mid-January, my counselor Dave and I sat down for an important discussion about my future. "What do you see for yourself as you get older Steve?", he asked me seriously.

Not sure of what my future held, I answered, "I really don't know Dave. What do you mean?"

"Well, obviously you can't stay here forever. What do you want to do from here?", he continued as I shrugged my shoulders. His voice and eyes showed genuine concern.

I was totally content in staying there at Harborcreek. I enjoyed being a freshman at the local high school. I was fine with my life just as it was.

Dave continued on, "Look, the staff and I have discussed it, and we think you may be better off in a foster home as opposed to staying here."

"Absolutely NOT Dave!", I snapped at him, "I've been down that road before. I don't want to be bounced around again. I like my school and I like my friends! I don't want to ruin that."

Dave looked at me for about a minute before suggesting, "What if we could find you a foster home right nearby?", he waited for my reaction, "That way you could still go to the same school? What would you say then?"

I thought for a moment before answering, "Maybe. Could I meet the family before making up my mind?", I asked.

"Absolutely!", Dave said with confidence, "I will try to get it set up. Then we can take it from there, okay?"

"Alright Dave, but if I don't like them, I'm not doing it!", I said with a very serious look in my eye.

"Sure buddy, I don't blame you.", he patted my back, "It'll work out, you'll see!"

A few weeks later, I went to spend the weekend with my possibly future foster family. They were "The Shafers". They lived just a few miles away. Just down the road from Harborcreek High. There were Glenda and Charles, the parents, and three kids. Jon and Ginger were twins and Chuck. All three of them went to my school. Chuck was one year older than me, Ginger and Jon were three years older.

Immediately I loved all of them. Glenda was very sweet. She had the softest eyes that I had ever seen. She insisted that I called her 'Mom', which I did. Actually everyone did. All of the neighborhood kids did as well. Charles was OK too, although he stayed quiet most of the time. I got along great with the other kids. We spent the weekend doing normal family stuff. We ate our meals as a family, and we went out to the mall and movies. By the time the weekend was over, my head was spinning. I loved this place. The Shafers shared my feelings and said they would be happy to have me living in their home full time. It was expected that this would take a few weeks or so, but in the meantime I could see them on weekends.

I went back to Harborcreek with really great news. I was getting to go and live with a family that I actually liked. Finally, I thought, my life was finally coming together. I called my mom to let her know what was happening, and she thought it was good too.

The first week of March 1990, I left Harborcreek to move in with the Shafer Family full time.

THE SHAFER RESIDENCE: HARBORCREEK, PA MARCH 1990

Glenda picked me up and brought me home with her. I got myself situated in my new bedroom, which I shared with Jon. We all had dinner together that first day and I was happy. For the first time in my entire life, I felt complete. I felt like I was really a part of this family. They loved me like I was one of their own. Glenda was the perfect 'mom'. I totally understood why everyone called her that. It was her role, and she played it so well. We would sit for hours talking about my life. When I told her my entire life story, she was floored.

"Well kiddo, I am SO sorry that you had to go through all of that.", her eyes were watery from tears, "We will take care of you though!", she hugged me, "We love you!"

"I love you too Mom!", I hugged her back. I did love her! She was great.

I continued to go to school at Harborcreek High. My new routine was very satisfying for me. I would hang out with Chuck after school, and on the weekends we would go and do normal kid stuff. I was at the top of my own new world. There was nothing that could bring me down. I finally had a home that I was happy in!

It was in late May that everything changed, and once again, my world crumbled before my very eyes.

Since I was from Lehigh County, and no longer in the Harborcreek Boys Home, I would be better off in a foster home closer to my own county.

Glenda tried to explain it to me, "They are going to take you back to Eastern Pennsylvania Steven. Closer to your family.", she said in tears.

"I don't want to go!", I protested.

"We don't want you to go either. But it's not up to us!", she continued, "Don't you worry though, we'll find a way to get you back. I promise.", she paused for a deep breath and continued with a set of words that I would remember for the rest of my life:

"By hook or by crook, we will get you back!"

That was the end of it. A few days later I was sitting in the back of a Sheriff's car headed East on Interstate 80. Only this time I wasn't cuffed or shackled. I hoped that the Shafers would find a way to get me back. I put my faith in them to take care of it.

THE YERGMAN RESIDENCE: BETHLEHEM, PA
JUNE 1990

After a few weeks in a children's shelter, I was placed with the Yergman family. They had a quaint little house on the outskirts of Bethlehem, in an area known as Steel City, due to its proximity to the Bethlehem Steel Mill which was nearby. The Yergmans were an older couple. Leslie, the mom was in her early fifties, and Frank, the dad was about the same age. They had two children, Ryan and Tricia. Ryan was home from college for the summer, and Tricia had just graduated high school. They seemed pleasant enough, but my heart was on the other side of the state. I was really banking on eventually being about to return to the Shafer's house as soon as I could.

The Yergmans were pretty lax when it came to house rules. They let me come and go as I pleased. After I was there for about a week, they took me up to the Pocono Mountains for a camping trip. They had a camper which we towed up and stayed in for about five days. I tried to enjoy myself, but I really wasn't into being out in the woods.

When we returned from the mountains, Ryan took me out to Kutztown University, where he went to college, for the weekend. He showed me around his campus and turned me onto a whole new music scene. He put me on to a band that I had never heard of before, The Cure. I was immediately pulled into their dark lyrics, and off key melodies. I had been in a kind of depressed funk since I had to leave Erie, so this music was perfect for me. I also began to write poetry. I would just sit in my room with the music blasting on my Walkman, a notebook in my lap and a pen in my hand, scribbling poem after poem. Pouring my words of sadness out on page after page.

I met a local girl named Stephanie, and the two of us hit it off pretty well. She was one year older than me, and she was gorgeous. She shared my affinity for poetry and depressing music. We could sit for hours sometimes, just listening to our music and reading each other's poems. Steph and I became inseparable. I would often sleep at her house and not even bother calling the Yergmans. We would share the same bed, and no one seemed to mind. Well, no one except the Yergmans. After I stopped showing up for a few days at a time, they got pretty irritated with me. I walked in the house one day after being gone for three, and Leslie was sitting at the kitchen table waiting for me.

"Where have you been, young man?", she asked me. Sitting there in her flowered housecoat, a cigarette hanging from her lips.

"I was at Steph's, Why?", I answered with the tone of a spoiled child, "As long as you get your check for me staying here, what does it matter?", a devilish look on my face.

She just stared at me in awe, "What do you mean get a check?", she questioned me. Apparently thinking that I had no idea how these things worked.

"You are getting paid to have me live here!", I retorted.

"What? How can you say such a thing?", she spoke back, trying to be dramatic.

I was well aware that foster parents were given money to take in kids. I also knew that the money was for more than it would cost to feed and clothe a child. There was enough for the family to have some left over. They were making a profit. Apparently Leslie thought I was just the average fourteen year old. Ignorant to the way the world worked.

"Listen lady, I have been in this juvenile system for over four years. Don't think for one minute that I don't know how it works!", I yelled in anger.

"You are a sick little child!", she yelled, "Now I want you to go to your room!", pointing to the stairs.

"Yeah right!", I responded and walked right out the front door.

I went back to Steph's house and told her what happened with Leslie. She just hugged me and sat me down on the couch in her embrace.

"Listen babe, I am here for you. You can stay here as long as you want.", she gave me a soft kiss, "I already talked to my mom and she said you can crash."

I kissed her back and responded, Thank you, but I can't stay forever. I just need to settle down for a while."

"Well whatever you want to do, I'm here!", smiling her angelic smile, "My home is your home."

I stayed for a few more days and then went back to the Yergmans. They weren't very happy when I walked in the door. I just sat down at the table and looked at both of them with rebellious eyes. I knew they had grown tired of me. I really didn't care. I had been in a happy home and was taken away. So, I made it a point to love my own way, no matter where I was or what the consequences were. I believed in my heart that I would eventually be about to return to the Shafers, so anything in the meantime was just a layover for me. They just stared at me for about a minute.

"What?", I snapped, "Why are you staring at me like that?"

"I think that we need to have a talk Steven.", Frank said sternly, "Your future here in this house is very questionable at this point." Leslie just sat there while her husband preached, "I think that you…"

"You want me to leave?", I cut him off before he could finish his words, "Fine, I will leave!", I barked as I stood up and headed to the door.

"Steven, wait!", Leslie pleaded, "You can't just leave like this."

I ignored her and continued out the door. I knew that they would call someone to let them know that I had left, but I didn't care. I just wanted to get out of there. I went back to Steph's and explained the situation to her and her mother. They listened intently as I explained the severity of the situation. When I was finished, Steph's mom asked with concern,

"What are they going to do to you?", her eyes showing deep concern, and her voice gentle.

"They will probably call my probation officer.", I responded.

"What does that mean for you?", Steph asked with a scared voice.

"They will probably come looking for me to take me away somewhere.", I explained, "They might send the police for me to lock me up again. I really don't know."

Steph's mom looked at me for a moment before speaking. I could tell from her eyes that she didn't want to be involved with the police.

"Listen sweetheart, I don't mind if you stay here for a night or two, but I can't have the police knocking on my door looking for you.", she said in a timid voice.

"I understand.", I said to her, "I will be out of your hair in the morning!"

"What are you going to do?", Steph asked me with both a frightened voice and eyes.

"I'm not sure. I will figure it out though.", I gave her a hug and kiss, telling her, "I will be fine, don't worry!", trying to console her.

The next morning I left and started to make my way toward Allentown. I decided that I was going to go and knock on my father's door and see what his reaction would be. As I was walking through Bethlehem, I spotted a car with its window down and no one in it. As I looked in the window, I saw a small wad of money in the center console. Looking around to see if anyone was looking, I decided that I would need money for my journey. I reached inside to grab it, and as I was pulling my arm out, someone yelled from across the street,

"Hey, what are you doing in my car?", the voice bellowed

I started to run, but the guy caught up with me and tried to grab me. He grabbed a hold of my backpack, and I turned around and kicked him in the nuts. He didn't let go of the backpack, but I slipped out of it and continued running. I hailed a cab to take me to my dad's.

When the cab dropped me off, I paid the driver with my ill gotten money and got out. I stood at the front door of my old apartment building for a few minutes deciding if I should ring the buzzer. When someone came out the front door, I slipped inside and took the elevator upstairs. I walked down the hallway to the apartment and found that the door was open a crack. I stuck my head inside and saw that it was empty. There were drop cloths on the floor and the whole place smelled of fresh paint.

"Hello?", I yelled, "Anyone here?", curious to why the place was empty.

A man came out from the back room. He was wearing coveralls with paint splattered all over them. "Can I help you?", he looked at me curiously.

"Yeah", I said, "Where is the guy that lived here?"

"Moved out a few weeks ago.", the painter answered, "Never even told anyone he was leaving."

"So, I'm guessing that he didn't leave any sort of an address?", I asked, waiting for the obvious answer.

"Um, No! He definitely didn't.", he answered as he pointed toward my old bedroom, "But he did leave some belongings, mostly kid stuff though. Was he your old man?", he asked.

"Yeah, how did you know?", I responded.

"I could tell by the look on your face. You can go and look around if you want. Take whatever you want. It's probably all yours anyway.", he said.

"Thanks, I won't be long.", I said as I walked to my old bedroom. When I walked in the room, I was shocked. Dad had left everything just as it was. He didn't take any of my things with him. All of the new clothes and stuff I had bought with the check money were still in the closet just as I had left them. I grabbed a duffel bag and put some clothes and stuff in it. I popped open the speaker of my stereo and saw that the money that had stashed it in almost two years before was still there. I grabbed the money and left the apartment without a word.

It didn't take long for the police to catch up to me for my theft from the stranger's car. He had my backpack and there were things with my name and address on them. Once they had my name, and realized I had left the Yergmans, they issued a warrant for me and picked me up late that night walking down Seventh Street in Allentown.

I was taken to the newly reopened Lehigh County Juvenile Detention Center to await my fate. I knew that the court would really be fed up with me now. I didn't care. I'd had enough of this whole thing. I would let them do whatever they were going to do. Nothing mattered to me anymore.

LEHIGH COUNTY JUVENILE DETENTION CENTER: ALLENTOWN, PA JULY 1990

Here I was. Locked up once again. The victim of my own stupid actions. Once I sat locked up for a few days, my rebellious attitude was replaced with one of fear. I knew that I was wearing out my welcome in the Pennsylvania juvenile system. I figured that the court would not go lightly on me. I felt like I was lost again. I had tried everything in the past. I tried it their way. I tried it my way. I behaved. I misbehaved. It seemed like no matter what I did, I was still given the shaft in the end. Sure, I didn't have to break the law. I didn't have to run away, and I didn't have to act out in my new foster home.

But, what no one else could seem to realize was that I was still a child. A child screaming out at the world for help. For love. Was I to blame for everything that happened? The judge seemed to think so. When I went to court and stood before him, he looked down at me from the bench and asked,

"Young man, why is it that no matter where you seem to go, you are followed by trouble?"

"I don't know Your Honor.", I answered with my usual shoulder shrugging, "I guess that I can't seem to find myself."

"Well son, I am going to give you a chance to find yourself.", he took off his glasses and stared intently at me, "I am going to give you a choice of where you are going to. I am going to give you one last chance to get your life together."

I looked at him and said, "Yes Your Honor."

"You have two options.", holding up two fingers and counting them off one at a time as he spoke, "Option one is that you go to the New Castle Maximum Security Center until you are eighteen years old.", he paused to see what my reaction was before continuing, "Option two is that you go to the Tressler Wilderness school until such a time that it is determined that you are ready to re-enter society."

I stared at him with an extremely puzzled look on my face. I didn't want to go to either place. I damn sure didn't want to be in a maximum security juvenile prison. But I also didn't like the idea of this wilderness thing.

The judge interrupted my stare, "Son, I am waiting to hear your answer."

"Um, Your Honor, I guess that I will have to choose the wilderness thing.", I answered quietly.

"That was a wise choice. I want you to use this opportunity to get your life together Son. I don't, I repeat, I DO NOT want to see you in my courtroom again. Do you understand me, young man?", he said with a very harsh tone of voice.

"Yes, Your Honor, I understand.", I responded, "I understand."

"Well, then, that is it. I hereby sentence you to the custody of the Tressler Wilderness School until such a time that it is determined that you are ready to be released back into society.", He tapped his gavel and I was taken from the courtroom to await my transfer to Tressler.

TRESSLER WILDERNESS SCHOOL: BOILING SPRINGS, PA AUGUST 1990

Tressler was located outside of Harrisburg, PA, at the foot of the Appalachian Mountains, which run from Maine to Georgia. It was really out in the middle of nowhere. As the sheriff's car bounced down the long dirt road, I began to wonder if I had made the right decision in choosing this place. I was in the middle of a forest with nothing on either side for miles but trees, trees, and more trees. At the end of the road, the car came to a stop in front of a large log cabin building. I was taken inside, where my cuffs and shackles were removed. After the sheriffs gave some man my paperwork, they left. I was standing there in the cabin which had been transformed into an office with a man staring at me. He stuck out his hand and introduced himself.

"My name is Warren Verner, I am the Director of Tressler.", he had a rather brash way about him. I reached out and shook his hand.

"I'm Steve.", was my only response.

"Well, Steve, why don't you come on into my office and I will explain our program to you.", he walked me toward an office in the back of the cabin. As we were passing another office, I noticed a cute blond secretary sitting at her desk. She smiled at me as I passed by, I smiled back.

"Have a seat.", Mr. Verner directed me to a chair. As I sat down, he continued, "Tressler is a place for you to challenge yourself. We will give you all of the tools that you will need to stretch yourself to the limits of your full potential……", he voice trailed off as I lost interest. I sat there thinking, 'Yeah dude, I get it, Wilderness, Cabin, Camping, Sure…Whatever!'

When he was done talking he asked, "Do you have any questions?"

"Um, no. I think I get the overall picture.", I answered.

"OK, good. I will get someone to show you around the camp. Have a seat in here.", pointing to another room.

He walked out of the cabin, and off into the woods. I looked around and saw pictures on the walls of people in canoes and climbing rock faces. As I glanced I was looking to see if there was an 'Uncle Sam I WANT YOU' poster lurking around. I walked over to the window to look out at the forest I was stuck in.

"Pretty peaceful isn't it?", a squeaky female voice came from my right. I turned to see the secretary standing beside me. "It really is a beautiful view, huh?", she continued.

"Yeah, it sure is.", I smiled as I looked her up and down. She noticed my look, but didn't say a word about it.

"I'm Joyce.", she said softly as she held out her hand.

"Steve.", I responded. Taking her hand gently and shaking it.

"Nice to meet you Steve!", she winked and walked off. She didn't look to be any older than twenty. It later turned out that she was actually only eighteen.

A few minutes later, a gangly kid with blond hair walked in the front door and approached us.

"You must be the new guy? I'm Scott.", he said as he extended his hand.

"Steve.", I responded, shaking his hand.

I spent the next hour getting my personal tour. There were four cabins for us to sleep in. Each one had between four and six sets of bunk beds. There was a bathhouse down a trail from the cabins where we could shower and use the bathroom. Down another trail, there was a set of double wide trailers that contained the school and chow hall. Other than that, there was a greenhouse at one end of a large grass clearing, and a wood shop at the top of the hill. I let out a sign as I looked around.

"What do we do when we're not in school?, I asked Scott.

"Not too much man!", he looked at me with a blank stare.

"Is there a TV or anything?", I asked.

"There is, but we really don't get to watch it.", he said as we walked back down the trail to the office cabin.

He pointed to another building off in the distance. "That's the property building where they keep all of our stuff that they don't want us to have.", Scott stated plainly.

"What do you mean 'don't want us to have'??", I asked.

"They'll go through your things and make sure that you don't have any contraband like jewelry, radios or cigarettes. Stuff like that.", he explained like I was some sort of idiot.

"Oh!", I responded. The only thing I could think of was that I wouldn't be able to have any of my music.

I worked my way into the normal daily schedule of Tressler. School in the daytime, and NOTHING in the evening. We got up at the crack of dawn for breakfast every morning. Lunch was at noon sharp. Dinner at five. I would normally spend my evenings sitting on a big rock outside of one of the cabins with my notebook writing my poems. The other kids kept their distance. They could tell that I wasn't interested in getting to know them. They could also tell that I wasn't interested in being there.

About two months after I got there, I was really fed up with being in the woods. Apparently, I wasn't alone. Me and two other kids made plans to escape. One night when the time was just right, we climbed out the cabin window and made our way through the woods to the main road leading to the school. Once we made it into town a few hours later, one of the kids hot-wired a car and drove us to Gettysburg. Both of the other kids were from that area. They decided to stay there, and I took the car to head to the only place that I could think of, The Shafers.

ON THE ROAD HOME: GETTYSBURG TO ERIE, PA OCTOBER 1990

I drove all day. Making my way through Central Pennsylvania, and West to Interstate 79. I followed I-79 North until I was arriving in Erie shortly after five in the evening. Just as I got near my old high school, the car ran out of gas. I pushed it to the side of the road and began to walk the rest of the way.

When I walked in the backdoor, the room fell silent. Mom and Ginger just stared at me in awe. Mom got up and came over to hug me.

"Steven, what in the hell are you doing here?", she exclaimed

"Not yet.", I said as we hugged. Not ready to let go.

After our embrace I sat down and told them everything that had happened since I left them. From the Yergmans all the way up to Tressler. I told them about my dad splitting, and about what the judge had said to me. They listened intently as I explained it all.

"So, what are you going to do now?", Ginger asked. She looked at mom, "Can he stay here?"

"We'll see.", mom looked at me with concern in her soft eyes. Concern that only a mother can have. "We'll see."

She made me a huge dinner, and after, I took a long shower. I began to head upstairs to lay down for a while. Mom said as I was heading up the stairs,

"Go on and get some rest. We'll talk more about this later on.", she winked at me as I smiled.

"Love you Mom!", I said as I went up.

"Love you too kiddo!", she replied.

That night, I slept better than I had in months. I slept from seven in the evening, all the way up until ten in the morning. I awoke with a smile on my face as I realized that I was truly home. I was looking forward to starting the first day of the rest of my life.

"Good morning kiddo.", Mom said as I walked into the kitchen yawning. "Did you sleep well?", she inquired. Charles was sitting at the table with a solid look on his face.

"Like a baby Mom!", I looked at Charles, "Good morning!", I shook his hand, "How've you been?", I asked.

"I've been fine. Listen, sit down for a minute, will you?", he said, gesturing toward an open seat. "I want to talk to you." Mom sat off to the side with a disapproving look toward Charles.

I sat down, "Sure, what's up?" in a plain voice.

"How did you get up here to Erie?", Charles asked rather curiously.

"Someone I was with took a car and gave it to me to drive up here.", I answered.
"So, you stole a car?", he asked.

"Well, I didn't actually steal it, but yeah, I suppose.", I stated.

"And where is this car now?", he interrogated.

"It ran out of gas by the high school. I walked the rest of the way.", I answered matter of factly.

Mom chimed in, "Look Charles, we will figure this out. Stop questioning him like he is a hardened criminal!", her voice in a protective tone.

"Glenda, he is a fugitive, and he has a stolen car.", he looked at her menacingly, "WE are the ones that can get in real trouble here!", Charles ranted.

"CHARLES!!", Mom yelled, "Calm down!"

He looked at me, "Look Steven, you know that we love to have you here, but it can't be like this.", he paused, "I am going to give you a few days to get your head together, and then I want you to move on.", and with that, he walked out of the room.

I wanted to cry. I looked at mom for some support. She just stared at me, and took a breath, "Look Steven, maybe you should just turn yourself in.", she said as the tears filled my eyes.

"I don't want to go mom.", I said in response, "What if they lock me up forever now?"

"I don't want you to go either.", she said, "But maybe if you turn yourself in, and I talk to the people at the wilderness place, they will take you back?", she waited to see how I took it.

"Can I stay for a few days before I do it?", I asked.

"Of course you can dear.", she held me tight to her chest, "Of course you can."

A few days later, mom drove me to the State Police barracks and I turned myself in. I was placed in the Edmund L. Thomas Juvenile Detention Center to await transfer back to Tressler. No charges were pressed against me for the car, and Tressler agreed to take me back. The other two kids were arrested before I turned myself in, but they were not taken back to Tressler. I was given a second chance to get it right. Mom told me that she was going to try to see if I could come and live with them when I got out.

BACK IN THE WOODS: TRESSLER WILDERNESS SCHOOL NOVEMBER 1990

I went back with the thought of being able to return to the Shafers when I completed the program. I volunteered to help in any fashion that I could to help around the camp. I'd often offer to help the cook, Bill, make lunch and dinner. I began to concentrate on my schooling. I continued to write my poetry in the evenings. I really wasn't punished for taking off. After I was back for about a week, it was as though it never happened.

Since I was spending so much time around the kitchen, Bill and I got pretty close. He was a huge Grateful Dead fan. Complete with the tye-dye t-shirts, and bushy beard. He looked after me like a father figure. Like Christine before him, Bill offered to take me home with him to spend the holidays with his family. Of course, I accepted.

I thoroughly enjoyed myself in Bill's home. I met his wife and two young children. They bought me a few Cure tapes for Christmas and my fifteenth birthday which had just passed. When I went back to the school, Bill snuck me in a walkman to listen to my tapes. I made sure to hide it well from the other staff. One of the counselors, Brad, discovered me with it one day, but when he saw what I was listening to, he just smiled and walked off without a word. Apparently, he was a fan too.

I began to learn more about nature and survival in the woods. Tressler actually had two parts. There was the wilderness school, which I was in, and the Tressler Survival Course. The survival course was a thirty day journey on the Appalachian Trail where you would really learn about survival and overcome the extreme nature of such things as hiking, rock climbing, and white water canoeing.

The survival course took you from Pennsylvania all the way to Georgia. Some kids were sentenced by judges to just the thirty day course. Others were sentenced to the school. Normally, kids sentenced to the school had to complete the thirty day course first. Somehow I fell through the cracks, so by the time I actually did my course, I had been there at Tressler for about six months. Not counting my short absence on the run. Everyone who completed the course was granted a leave for a week to spend with their families. Bill and I made plans for me to go and stay with him upon completion of my thirty days. It would be my inspiration to get through the rigors of the course.

The day before I left for my journey, I got a letter from Christine. I had called her when I ran from the woods, and when I got back to Tressler, I wrote her a letter to let her know that I had turned myself in. She wrote back saying that she was proud of me for turning myself in and facing the challenges that awaited me. That provided me with a boost of confidence.

30 DAYS ON THE APPALACHIAN TRAIL: PENNSYLVANIA TO GEORGIA FEBRUARY 1991

The rigors of hiking up to twenty miles a day was daunting at first. I couldn't imagine that I would survive the thirty days. I pushed myself harder than I ever thought I could. There were about fifteen other kids on the course with me, along with three instructors.

We were taken through the basic parameters of surviving in the wilderness. A lot of the things that were taught to us, I had already learned throughout my time in the school. Which gave me a leg up on most of the other kids. The instructors knew that I was more knowledgeable in these aspects, so they looked to me to be a sort of mentor to the other kids. I tried my best to help in any way I could. The only thing I wanted was to get through this and get on with my visit to Bill and his family. I was also planning on using the completion of the course as a stepping stone to go back and live with the Shafers.

It was frigid in the woods. We slept in special sleeping bags to keep us warm at night. There were no actual tents, just big blue tarps tied to trees overhead. Each day we would cook a dinner consisting of high protein and high carb meals. A lot of beans and noodles. The food was cooked in a large pot directly on the campfire. There were no luxuries out there. If you had to use the bathroom, you dug a hole and used leaves to wipe.

Before I knew it, we were in the mountains in Georgia. Almost three weeks had passed and I was getting along just fine with everything. We left the mountains and canoed on the Flint River for almost a week. We would paddle for about twenty miles everyday. Stopping at night, and making camp on the banks of the river.

Following the canoeing was a three day 'Solo Course'. The solo course was to test your learning of survival. Each of us was blind folded and walked into a section of the woods to our own little area. We were given three matches, one water bottle, three packs of oatmeal, three packs of ramen noodles, a sheet of plastic to make a tarp, and a small metal cooking pot. We kept our sleeping bags to sleep in. The instructors walked us one by one to our areas. They showed us the boundaries of our campsites and left us there. We each had a journal and a small pencil to write what we were feeling during our solitude. There was a small stream by the site to get water from. There was nothing around for miles. I couldn't see anybody else's site, they couldn't see me. I was alone. But that was the point.

The first day, I set up my tarp and slept. I was in dire need of sleep. I got my fire going just before the sun went down, and made myself a dinner of ramen noodles. It rained horrendously that first night. The small plastic tarp was useless. I took it down and wrapped it around the sleeping bag. At the very least my body was dry.

Day two brought beautiful sunshine. I gathered some firewood and laid it out on the rocks at the bank of the stream to dry in the sun. A few hours later I started my fire and made some oatmeal. I spend the rest of the day just scribbling in my journal. Writing poems and other mindless dribble. I slept well the second night. It was so nice out that I didn't even need the tarp up. I decided to instead lay there and look at the stars.

By day three, I was ready to get back to the finish of my course. I began to get extremely bored. I tried to nap, but couldn't. I tried to write, but couldn't. I ate the rest of my food, and made sure that my fire would burn through the night. When the instructors came to get me in the morning. I ran to them like I had been lost on Gilligan's Island. It was great to see someone, anyone.

The only thing left to do was a twenty kilometer run. Well, that and the almighty ropes course. I made it through the run with no problem. When we all completed the run, we were taken in the van back to Pennsylvania to do the ropes course.

The ropes course rivaled an Army boot camp course. There was climbing, rappelling and even a tightrope walk. All of these things were upward of fifty feet in the air. There were safety nets of course, as well as ropes and harnesses tied to us. But it was still a challenge to mostly everyone. The course was on the grounds of Tressler and I had been through it many times before. I really didn't have any problems. With that done, we were on our last night of the thirty days. We had a huge feast, and got our third shower in a month.

The next day there was a graduation ceremony for all of us. Most of the kids had their families there. I had Bill. When the ceremony was over, all the kids went home. Bill took me out to lunch and back to Tressler. It was planned that the next weekend he would take me home with him for two weeks. I got situated back in my cabin and actually missed being out there on the course. Even though I was in the woods, I missed the woods. It was hard for me to sleep on a mattress.

A part of me really changed over that month. I realized that I could do things that I never thought I could. I had challenged myself and overcome that challenge. I felt like I could handle anything after that. I felt like I could move a mountain. Little did I know that I would be given another challenge, only this one I would fail miserably at.

A TREE FALLING IN THE WOODS: TRESSLER
MARCH 1991

On the second night back in the camp after my course, an event happened that would lead to my self-destruction. One of the other kids decided it would be amusing to break into the supply room of the chow hall. The only thing he took was a case of Snickers bars.

The next morning, when the staff had discovered the break in, they put the entire camp in a frenzy. We were all taken to the chow hall while the staff searched the cabins for the missing items. About an hour later, the Director, Mr. Verman came into the chow hall to address the camp.

"Gentleman, I am sure by now you are aware of what happened last night.", he paced back and forth in front of us, "and you know that this type of mischief will not be tolerated in this camp.", he glared at each of us with a discerning eye, "Furthermore, I have decided that since there were people in the cabin with the culprit who allowed him to leave in the middle of the night, and return with this…", holding up the case of candy bars up, "…That all of you will be made to pay for his actions.", he pointed to a kid that I had never even seen before.

He went on, "This camp is now on freeze. That means no activities, no free time, and for those of you who have home visits scheduled, you WILL NOT be going. You can all thank this young man right here!, he pointed at the kid and left.

I was beside myself with anger. I looked around to see that everyone else was too. This new kid had just ruined my scheduled visit at Bill's. I had busted my ass for thirty days in the woods only to have some stranger take my prize from me. There was no way that I could allow this deed to go unpunished.

Later that night, me and a few other kids followed him down to the bathhouse. Inside the bathhouse there was a hot water heater in a cage in the far corner. It was locked with a small padlock. We walked in after the kid, and beat the hell out of him. I picked the lock, and we put him in the cage and left him there bloody and bruised.

The other kids had put their winter ski masks on to protect their identities from him, but I wanted him to look me right in my eyes. I wanted him to know how bad his actions had fucked up my plans. I wanted him to suffer in that cage. Just like I was suffering not being able to take part in the small amount of freedom that I had worked so hard for.

The next morning, one of the staff found the kid locked in the cage and let him out. He made it a point to let them know that I was the ringleader of his punishment. I was called to see the Director and he was none too happy to learn of my deed.

"Steven, what were you thinking?", he asked.

I just looked at him like he was nuts. I felt totally justified in my actions. I felt that deep down, they wanted us to punish him. Why else would they make all of us suffer for his actions? Why did he make it a point to let everyone know who had done it by pointing him out to all of us?

"Are you going to answer me?", he barked.

"You are the one who made it a point to tell us that he did it, and that we were going to suffer.", I barked back, and glared at him. "Did you really think that one of us wasn't going to do something to the kid?"

"Well, I sure as hell didn't expect this", he exclaimed, "Now I want to know who was with you last night! I want to know who your accomplices were!"

"I had no accomplices.", I stated coyly, "I was all alone."

"I was told that there were four of you.", he went on, "Now who were the others?"

"It was JUST me!", I gave him a menacing grin.

He shuffled some papers on his desk and looked up at me. "You don't want to tell me, fine. But, I want you to know that I am calling the probation office to let them know that YOU did this all by yourself.", he adjusted his glasses so he could look over the rims at me, "Now go back to your cabin!", he yelled and pointed at the door.

I knew what this meant for me. They were going to kick me out. I would have to go back in front of that judge. He was going to lock me up for the next three years. I knew that if I didn't run that night, the next day I would be leaving in handcuffs and shackles. I formulated a plan in my head and when it got dark out, I set it into motion. I told the three kids from the night before what had happened. I explained to them that I would have to leave that night. They knew that I didn't give them up. In return for my silence, they assisted me in my escape.

MY DARING ESCAPE FROM THE WOODS: MARCH 1991

When the time was right, I ran down the trail to the office cabin. I climbed in the window and rutted around until I came across a one way bus ticket from Harrisburg to Allentown. There was also an envelope of petty cash which contained about thirty dollars. I took the ticket and the money and went back to the cabin to wait until the time was right to leave.

At about two in the morning, when everyone else was asleep, I crept out of my cabin and made my way to the property building. I got inside and kicked in the door to the property room holding everyone's stuff. I filled a duffel bag with everything of value that I could find. Walkmans, Gameboys, and a load of gold jewelry.

Most of the kids at Tressler were drug dealers, and a lot of them came with a good assortment of gold necklaces and rings. I figured I could sell the stuff for money if I needed to.

I went into the woods and began my journey. I needed to get to Carlisle, PA. Which was about 10 miles from where I was. There was a bus depot there that I could get a bus to Harrisburg to use the ticket I had taken. Since I had just spent so much time in the woods, I had no problem finding my way through the woods all the way to Carlisle. I didn't even walk on a road until I was just about a quarter mile from the bus depot. By the time I got on that bus to Harrisburg, they wouldn't even know I had left yet.

I got to Harrisburg with ease, and used my ticket to Allentown. Shortly before noon I was arriving in Allentown. I took a cab to Bethlehem and went to see Steph. I figured I could stay for a day or two and lay low.

Since I hadn't damaged anything in the office, and there were no home visits scheduled for anyone, I figured it would be a day or two before they discovered the missing ticket and money. I would be long gone from the Allentown/Bethlehem area by then.

Steph was very happy to see me. I told her what had happened and she said it probably wouldn't be a good idea for me to stay the night. But she made arrangements for me to stay with one of her friends. I needed to figure out where I could go. I couldn't, under any circumstances, go to the Shafers. I feared that the first place the authorities would look would be their house.

I decided to call my friend Justin in Middletown, New Jersey. He and I had kept in contact up until I went to Tressler, so I figured that maybe I could go and crash in Jersey at his house. I spoke with his mother and she informed me that he had moved to Buffalo, NY to live with his aunt. She asked me how I was, and I told her I was fine. I never let on about my current status, but I suspect that she might have had some sort of idea. She gave me his address in Buffalo, but claimed that she didn't have the phone number handy. I thanked her and told her I would drop him a line.

I decided that Buffalo would be a good place to hide. After all, no one knew that I knew anyone in Buffalo. I needed money though. I took a bus to Philadelphia to try to sell some of the jewelry and stuff. I sold everything with ease. I kept a walkman for my travels, and pocketed about three hundred dollars from my sale. I spent a few bucks on a legitimate looking Fake ID that said I was over eighteen. The name on the ID; 'Steven Shafer'!! I called Christine and confided in her what had happened. She just laughed on the phone. She told me to get to Erie and call her. I didn't say anything to her about Buffalo on the phone. I knew that Buffalo was close enough to Erie for me to get there easily. I got myself a one way ticket to Erie, and got on the bus. Twelve hours later, I arrived in Erie and called Christine.

Christine picked me up and was very happy to see me. She wasn't really pleased that I had gone and screwed up again, but she understood why I did it. She said that she wouldn't call the cops or anything. I told her of my plans to go to Buffalo, and she agreed that it would be good for me to go somewhere no one expected me to go.

Buffalo was my best bet. I stayed with her for a few days and she took me to the bus station so I could continue my travels. She made me promise to keep in touch. Which, of course I would. I was now on my way to start yet another new life. Even though it was a life on the run, I was confident that I could make it work. Buffalo, NY here I come!! I thought as the bus headed down the road.

FINDING A NEEDLE IN A HAYSTACK: BUFFALO, NY MARCH 1991

I had an address. That was it. Thirty five dollars, and an address in my pocket. I got off the bus in Buffalo and got a map of the city. I looked at the address that Justin's mom had given me; 42 Gates, Buffalo, NY. I looked up Gates on the map and found that it was actually Gates Circle. I hailed a cab to take me there. It was a straight shot down Delaware Avenue from the bus station. The cab dropped me off and I started to search for the address.

There was no such number on Gates Circle. I walked around the hare for about an hour to see if maybe I had written the number down wrong. But all of these numbers were in the hundreds and not one of them could have been confused with 42. Here I was in a strange city, with barely any money in my pocket, and nowhere to stay. I was tempted to get back on a bus and head back to Erie, but something in me said that I should stay and continue my search. So I did.

I made my way back to the bus station, since it was the only place that I knew I could mill around while figuring out my next move. Plus, there was heat inside. Buffalo in March can be mighty cold.

I met up with two girls named Michelle and Tracey at the bus station and they somehow could tell that I was kind of lost. They both were average looking, and seemed to be in their mid-twenties. Neither of them knew of the address that I had written down. They both lived near Gates Circle though, and gave me their number in case I needed help later on. After a few hours at the bus station I decided to give them a call to see if I could borrow their couch for the night to crash.

"No Problem.", Michelle said on the phone. She rambled off her address and asked, "Do you want one of us to come and meet you down there?"

"No, I will just grab a cab.", I responded and hung up.

I made my way to their apartment and when Tracey opened the door, I could see a cloud of smoke in the living room. She exhaled and giggled as she let me in. I then realized it was pot smoke in the air. I definitely needed some of that right now.

Tracey and Michelle were both from the Syracuse area and were going to College in Buffalo. They got me stoned and we all just sat up most of the night having fun. As we were passing around a joint, Michelle asked,

"So, Steve, where are you from?", her voice raspy from the smoking.

"Jersey.", I replied as I exhaled. My head spinning from the effects of the pot.

"JOISEY!", They both yelled and started to laugh.

"What's wrong with that?", I asked in contempt.

"Oh, nothing. It's just that Tracey here used to date a guy from Jersey.", Michelle said.

"Yeah, and he had the most annoying accent.", Tracey chimed in, "I hated that accent. But you don't seem to have it Stevie. Why is that?", she winked her eye at me and the two of them began to giggle again.

"Well, I have been living in Pennsylvania for the past few years, So I guess it kind of disappeared.", I replied after another hit.

"How old are you Steve?", Michelle asked me with a coy look on her face.

"Eighteen!", I replied, thinking of my fake ID.

"Wow, we both thought you were at least twenty!", Michelle said, grinning at me again.

"Yeah, you look older!", Tracey offered.

You have no idea! I thought! We continued to roll and pass joints around to each other. Then Michelle jumped up and screamed,

"Who wants to take a shower?, as she ran toward the bathroom.

"Oh, I do!", Tracey followed, "Come on Stevie.", she grabbed my hand and pulled me down the hall.

I had never showered with one, let alone two women before. I hadn't done much with a woman at all. Everything changed that night. Tracey passed out on the couch. But Michelle took me into the bedroom, and although she didn't know it, she took my virginity from me. It was turning out that Buffalo might be alright after all. Whether I found Justin or not.

The next thing I remember was waking up in the bedroom the next morning completely clueless as to where I was. After getting my bearings, I noticed that Michelle was still asleep. I went to the bathroom to take another shower. This one by myself. When I came out, Tracey was waking up on the couch.

"Hey", she said with a groggy voice. "What time is it?", she rubbed the crust from the corners of her eyes.

"Almost nine thirty.", I replied.

"Shit, I missed my first class!", she said as she jumped up. "Is Michelle up?", I shook my head No.

She went into the bedroom to wake her roommate and I plopped down on the couch. The two of them came a few minutes later and Tracey gave me the 'All Knowing' look. The two of them grabbed some books and bags and made their way to the door.

"Steve, feel free to hang out until we get back. We should be in by noon.", Michelle said. She gave me a quick peck on the lips and the two of them were gone.

I looked around at the sparsely furnished apartment. There was an entertainment center with a TV and stereo, a leather footstool in the corner, and a small glass coffee table in front of the sofa.

I reached for the telephone to try to call Christine to let her know that I had arrived in Buffalo, but there were no long distance calls allowed from their number. I looked up the address for a local library so that I could find out if this mystery address I had was real or not. I left the girls a short note saying that I would be back later and headed off to the library.

"Gates..Um..let me see here.", the woman at the reference desk said as she thumbed through a directory of street listings for the greater Buffalo area. "I only have two listings for Gates. There's Gates Circle here in the city."

"I have already been there, that's not it", I cut her off.

"And there is Gates Street in Sloan.", she continued, apparently annoyed at my interruption.

"Where is Sloan?", I asked.

"Just outside of the city. Here look..", she pointed to a street map, "Go straight down Broadway until it ends, and then make a right and you are in Sloan.", she offered.

"Can I possibly get a copy of that map?", I asked kindly.

"Sure, wait here.", she walked off for a minute, then came back and handed me the copy, "There you go!", I thanked her and left. I decided to wait until the next day before I went to find Justin. I went back to the girls apartment figuring they would be back from class by then.

"So, did you find your mystery street?", Tracey asked as I walked in the door. She was eating a bowl of cereal while looking intently at a textbook. Michelle was nowhere in sight.

"Yeah, I found it.", I answered as I looked around the room, "Where's Michelle?"

"She's with her boyfriend!", Tracey winked at me, "I heard you two had a little fun last night!"

Embarrassed, I sheepishly replied, "What did you hear?"

"Oh, you know what I heard.", she took another spoon of cereal. "Be careful though, her boyfriend is pretty big! And black.", she thought to add.

I wasn't sure how to take all of this. What the hell was this girl doing sleeping with me when she had a boyfriend? "Do you think she'll tell him about me?", I asked.

"Oh, he already knows about you, but he thinks that you and I are the ones who hooked up, so if he's around, you better make him believe it.", she blew a kiss and started to laugh.

"Oh Shit!", I said in a panic, "He's gonna kick the shit out of me!"

"No, he won't, calm down!", she said, "Here, smoke this!", she handed me a pipe packed with weed. "Just relax, I 'll help you out! IF, you help me out!", she laughed as I took a hit.

That's how it played out for me. I screwed Tracey during the afternoons while Michelle was with her boyfriend Tony, and in the evenings the four of us hung out together. Tony was oblivious to what had happened. He and I got along ok. Like me, he had a checkered past. He lived in the project in the 'Fruit Belt', a section of town just off the highway that came into the city. When he heard that I was from Jersey, he thought that was pretty cool.

A few days later I went out to search for my long lost friend Justin. When I found that house and knocked on the door, I didn't know what to expect. He opened the door and it took him a moment to recognize me. When it occurred to him who I was, he just started laughing.

"I knew it! I knew you were gonna show up here!", he said as he gave me a hug. "Here man, come on in! How in the hell have you been?", he directed me inside, ""WHERE in the hell have you been?"

"All over man! How did you know I was gonna show up here?", I questioned.

"My mother called me a few days ago, and told me that you called.", he laughed out the words, "She said that you were really curious to know where I was, and that when she said that I had moved up here, you acted kind of weird when you wanted the address. I just knew it! Where did you take off from this time?", he said with a huge grin.

"It's a long story man.", I replied with a sigh.

"Well, let's hear it! I've got plenty of time!", he walked to the kitchen and got us a drink.

I told him the whole story about all of the shit that had happened at Tressler and he took it all in as I spoke. I told him about Tracey and Michelle and the big, black boyfriend. By the time I was done talking, he just looked at me amazed.

"Dude, you have had the craziest life man.", he stated.

"You don't have to tell me. I'm the one living it.", was my only response. It felt kind of nice to have someone from my past to share my feelings with. It had been five years since Justin and I had met, and with all that I had been through since then, I was glad that he was there for me to listen.

Justin was still in high school, so I mainly got to see him in the evenings and the weekends. He told his aunt that he knew me from Jersey and that I was living in town with my dad. She really didn't seem to like me too much. I think that she knew of my ruse. She never interfered with our friendship though.

Before I knew it, I had been in Buffalo for more than a month. I was starting to grow more comfortable with my life on the run. I got a job bussing tables in a small Greek restaurant. They paid me under the table, so I was able to avoid showing any real proof of who I was. I continued to live with Tracey and Michelle. They would go to school during the daytime while I worked. When I wasn't with Justin, the girls and I would hang out in the evenings. Even though I was sleeping with Tracey, I wanted more of Michelle. Her boyfriend had been thrown in the county jail, so he wasn't around, which made me want her more.

Sometimes when Tracey was asleep or at one of her classes, Michelle and I would screw around. We tried to keep it a secret from Tracey. But she wound up walking in on us one day and the cat was out of the bag. The bad thing is that I was still screwing her too, just not as much as he would have liked I guess, because when she walked in the room, she was pissed. She took one look at us and slammed the door as she stormed back out of the house. We got up and tried to catch her, but she was gone. Michelle and I both felt a bit guilty. There really wasn't anything exclusive between Tracey and I, but just the fact that I was staying with them should have been enough for me to know better. But I was fifteen years old, what the hell did I really know? Michelle took it a little harder though, she was concerned that she would lose her friend over the whole thing.

What she wasn't worried about that she should have been, was her boyfriend. Even though Tony was in jail, he wound up finding out. I can't quite determine how he found out, but I would bet money on it being Tracey who told him.

About three weeks after catching the two of us in bed, Tracey said that Tony was out of jail. When I looked at her and asked how she knew, she looked at me and said,

"I know because I saw him last night!"

"Does Michelle know?", I asked.

"No, but she will soon enough.", she had a devilish grin on her face, "She will."

"What the hell is that supposed to mean?", I asked.

The only thing she had to say was, "You'll see!". I really didn't read too much into it at the time. I just shrugged and wound up leaving to go to work for the day. I finished my shift at the restaurant around six thirty and decided to head over to Justin's place. It was a Friday night, so I figured that rather than deal with the soap opera at my place, I would crash with Justin for the night. That night I told him about my little problem at home. He knew that I was sleeping with one of the girls, but when I told him that I had been doing both of them separately, he was shocked.

"No shit man. You have been screwing both of them?", he yelled out.

"Yeah, but I really screwed up bro. Now there is a whole jealous roommate thing going on. Plus there is the boyfriend that is supposedly out of jail.", I tried to explain to him, "What if he really IS out, and he comes after me?"

"How long has he been in jail?", Justin asked.

"A little over a month, Why?", I said with curiosity in my voice.

"If it's only been a month since he was locked up, then he is probably still there. Nobody gets out of jail in just a month.", Justin explained.

"What about my dad? He was only in jail for a few days.", I challenged.

"That is different. Your dad was an upstanding citizen. This Tony dude lives in the frigging projects. People like that don't get out that quickly. Don't you watch TV?", was his response which reeked of prejudice.

I thought about what he said, and merely replied, "Yeah, I suppose."

I let it go out of my head. I spent the rest of the weekend at Justin's and on Monday morning, when he went to school, I headed back to work. I hadn't been back to the girls apartment or called since the weekend began. I decided to give them a ring to let them know that I was at work and I would be back later.

"Hello", Tracey answered the phone.

"Hey, it's Steve, what's going on over there?", I asked.

"Oh, it's Steve, Hey Steve.", she said with a weird voice, "Steve, how are you? Where are you Steve?", in a voice eerily reminiscent of Crazy Betty from the in-patient unit from years ago.

Why the hell did she keep saying my name? I couldn't figure out what was going on. I heard the phone drop and someone yelling in the background. Michelle grabbed the phone from the floor and yelled in my ear,

"Steve, Tony's out and he knows everything!", her voice was panic stricken, "He's got a gun and he is coming to look for you at work. Get out of there now, and whatever you do, don't come back here.", she cried out, "He wants to kill you!"

I didn't wait for any more words to come from the other end of the phone. I hung up, grabbed my coat and left the restaurant without a word. I got in a cab and headed to the bus terminal. I got on the next bus headed for the only place I could think of, Erie. I didn't want to even want to wait to talk to anyone about the whole thing. I just left.

RUNNING WHILE ON THE RUN: ERIE, PA MID-APRIL 1991

During the two hour bus ride from Buffalo to Erie, I tried to make a plan of action. I was going to call Christine and ask if she could help me with a place to stay until I made other plans.

When I arrived, I got off the bus and headed to the mall to get lunch and use the phone. I had a burger and called Christine. There was no answer, so I decided to take a bus out to Harborcreek to see the Shafers. I figured that I had been out of the area long enough for any potential heat to die down. I got off the bus and went into a Burger that Glenda's son Jon was working at. He seemed really surprised to see me.

"Steve, what are you doing out here?", Jon asked as I approached the counter, "I heard that you disappeared from that wilderness place and vanished?"

"I did, but I wanted to come and visit you guys.", I looked at him and smiled, "How's Mom?"

"Um, she's fine….uh…where have you been at?", he had a weird look in his eyes.

"Up in Buffalo. I got a place to stay up there for a while.", I answered.

"Hey, have a burger or something on me.", he pointed over his shoulder to the menu on the wall. "I've got to clean up the back, and then I'm off. After I am done, I will drive you to the house."

"Ok, give me a number three combo.", I got my food and sat down at a table to wait for him to wrap up his shift.

About ten minutes later, I saw a State Police car pulling up to the building. This sort of thing was common out here, but I decided to get up and head to the bathroom and wait until they were gone. I walked in and opened a stall door and took a seat. A minute later I heard the bathroom door open and two sets of footsteps squeaking on the tile floor. The feet stopped in front of my stall and I could see the shiny boots. Boots that were easily recognized as belonging to a cop.

My heart started to thump in my chest. I felt the blood rushing to my ears as I looked down at the boots in front of the door. THUMP, THUMP, THUMP!   A series of knocks came to the stall door. THUMP, THUMP, THUMP!

"Um, someone's in here!", I said timidly, hoping that they would go to another stall, but knowing better.

"Steven, come on out. We're with the State Police and we know that you are in there.", the deep voice came from the other side of the door.

"I don't know what you're talking about. I'm just trying to use the bathroom. Don't know any Steven!", I responded.

"Look, we know who you are, and we are here to take you in. So come on out and let's get this over with.", the second voice chimed in.

I was caught. There was nowhere for me to run. There was nowhere for me to go. I had to come out and face the music. I opened the stall door and walked out. The cop looked at me and said,

"You ARE Steven, correct?", his voice confident, because he already knew the answer.

I sighed, and replied, "Yeah."

"Come on, you are under arrest. We have a warrant for you from Lehigh County.", he cuffed me, "We have to take you in, Let's go.", his voice gruff in my ears.

They walked me outside and put me in their cruiser. Once again, I was transported to the Edmund L. Thomas Juvenile Detention Center in Erie. Only this time my transfer wouldn't be back to Tressler. It would be back to Lehigh County to face the judge for the last time. I knew that all of my chances were gone. I was sure that I was going to be sent away for a long time now.

LEHIGH COUNTY
JUVENILE DETENTION CENTER:
ALLENTOWN, PA
APRIL 1991

The guards and the kids in the detention center didn't seem surprised to see me. Most of them knew that I had made a daring escape from Tressler. So, when I was caught and waiting in Erie to be transported back to Lehigh, they were waiting for my return. I got some cheers from the other kids. To them, I was like a special sort of criminal. Being on the run and getting away with it longer than most. To the guards, my exploits were a type of amusement. I would tell them stories of my journey and they would just laugh. Not really at me, but with me. The only thing was that both groups, kids and guards alike, also knew that I was going to be punished harshly for my deeds. This was kind of a disappointment to the guards. Most of them knew the stuff I had been through over the years, and they seemed to feel sorry for me. Even though I screwed up every chance that I was given, they all agreed with me that I usually got the worst of it all in the end. As I was sitting the day room one day talking to a guard, he said to me,

"Damn Steve, it's a shame that you can't just go back to your mother's in Jersey."

A light flashed in my brain, "What did you say?", I asked.

"I said that you should be able to go back to your mother's in Jersey.", he looked at me and followed up with, "Why? What did you think I said?"

"Um, Nothing.", I walked off. I went to sit down by myself to think. What he said to me gave me a brilliant idea. I could use it in my favor when I went to court.

My first court hearing was scheduled for May 6th. I was escorted into the courtroom in handcuffs. As I approached the bench, I felt confident for the first time. The judge glared down at me from his high bench.

"Well, look who it is. Why am I not surprised to see you back here so soon?", he said in an obvious tone.

"I don't know Your Honor, Why?", I responded with my eyes wide.

"I believe that the last time you were here, I told you that you were getting your last chance. Isn't that right?", he spoke with a confident tone.

"Yes Sir, you did.", I answered.

"And, I believe that I told you that I would lock you up until you were eighteen. Can you give me one good reason why I shouldn't do that?", the judge asked.

"Well, Your Honor, I just might be able to do that. But first I would like to ask you a question.", I said.

"Sure Son, you are entitled to speak.", he responded.

"Your Honor, what would happen if the court found out that my father, who is my legal guardian, by the way, no longer resided in Pennsylvania?", I asked with confidence.

"Well, let me see…", he put his hand to his balding head, "...then you would become a ward of the state.", he answered me.

"What if both of my parents shared custody over me, but my dad only had physical custody?", I asked.

"Son, what are you getting at?", the judge barked, "I don't have the time or patience for your games in my courtroom, so what is the point?"

"Your Honor, my father no longer lives in Pennsylvania. Both him and my mother share custody of me, and my mother lives in New Jersey.", I stated bluntly, "So my question is, what would the court do about that?"

The judge sat back for a moment and responded, "Well, if that WAS the case, then the court would have no choice but to put you in the other parent's custody."

"Well Your Honor, that is the case.", I said, as I looked up at him. Half smirk on my face.

"Where is the father?", he barked at my probation officer, "Does he still live here or not?"

"We have been unable to locate the father for some time now Your Honor.", my probation officer replied.

"Well, this is what we are going to do. We are going to ascertain whether or not the father lives here anymore, and then we are going to find out about the custody issue.", he yelled, and looked at me menacingly, "You had better not be wasting this court's time young man."

"I am not Sir.", I said fearlessly, "I'm sure if you look into the matter, you will see that what I am telling you is indeed the case Your Honor.."

"Very well then, this court is adjourned until such a determination is made.", he tapped his gavel and left the courtroom.

I was transported back to the detention center. If I had learned anything over the past five years in the system, it's who has what type of custody over me. It all dawned on me the day the guard said something about my mother. I coupled that with the knowledge that my dad had left the apartment.

Four days later, on May 10th, I was taken back in front of the judge. He had a slight grin on his face when I approached the bench.

"Young man, I have got to hand it to you. You seem to really know how to get yourself out of sticky situations.", he waved a piece of paper in the air, "What I have in my hands right here is a copy of your parents Divorce Decree. Do you have any idea what it says?", he asked.

"I believe that it says that both of my parents share custody of me.", I answered.

"Indeed it does.", he nodded his head, "Do you know what that means for this court?", he paused, "It means that you are no longer my problem. You are now the State of New Jersey's problem to deal with! I spoke with your mother a few minutes ago, and informed her that you would be coming to live under her roof.", his voice beamed across the room.

"I will? What did she have to say?", I asked.

"Well, she was completely surprised to say the least. How long has it been since you have seen her?"

"A few years ago, Your Honor.", my response was timid. I began to wonder what she would do with me. I decided to ask, "Your Honor, what if she is unwilling to take me?"

"She has no choice, Son. On Monday morning, the sheriffs will be taking you to your mother's house.", he responded, "I have already informed the probation department in New Jersey that you will be coming. This is truly the last chance that you will get. I hope that you use this to get your life together before it's too late!"

"I will Sir, Thank you.", I said proudly.

"Don't thank me. Thank the Divorce Attorney.", he continued, "If it were up to me, I would send you away right now. I do have to give you credit though. You were right, and you knew it. But next time, you might not be right. Then you will have to pay. Good Luck Son.", he stood up from behind the bench and walked into his chambers.

Three days later, the day after mother's day, I was picked up by the Lehigh County Sheriffs. I was finally getting a chance to live with my family. After five years of being bounced around from place to place, I was going home. I was determined to make it work this time!

COURT ORDERED PARENTING: MOM'S HOUSE HOWELL, NJ MAY 13, 1991

The sheriff's car pulled into the driveway of mom's split level ranch house on Bristlecone Drive and for the first time in years, I was almost at ease. I was sure that David didn't want me there, but the fact that mom was giving in and accepting me was gratifying. Even though she didn't have much of a choice in the matter.

I walked to the front door and rang the bell. Mom came out and gave me a big hug.

"You got so big!", she said as we hugged.

I looked up at David standing there in the doorway with an overwhelmed look on his face. "Steven, how are you?", he asked from the doorway.

"I'm fine David, how are you?", I responded. Extending my hand to shake his.

"Good, Come on in.", he answered, shaking my hand back. I could tell that he was putting on a show for me. Mom sat down in the kitchen and took a long look at me.

"How are you?", she asked .

"I'm OK Mom, I'm fine.", I looked at her seriously.

David sat down with us and leaned across the table. I could tell that he was going to say something to me that I didn't really want to hear.

"Listen Steven, this whole thing with you living here was thrown in our lap.", I nodded as he spoke, "I'm not sure if you realize this or not.", mom sat by while he preached on, "We have spoken to the people here in the local probation office, and we've decided to go along with this and give you a chance to prove yourself here."

I looked at him and said, "I understand.", trying to give him the most honest look that I could.

"Good, why don't you go and get yourself situated in your room. We have an appointment to meet your new probation officer in a few hours.", he said as he walked out of the kitchen.

I looked at mom and smiled. She smiled back, but I could tell by her face that she was a little fearful of how this whole thing would work out.

"Are you OK Mom?", I asked with concern.

"I'm fine Steven, this is just hard for us!", she patted my hand, "I'll be fine. Go and unpack.", she gave me a slightly limp grin.

My brother and sister were off at school. As I unpacked my things, I wondered if they knew that I was coming home. Sitting down on the bed, I looked around and felt like everything was going to be OK.

A few hours later the three of us got into mom's new car and went to Freehold to the county courthouse to meet my new probation officer. Mom and David went in first, and after about twenty minutes, I went in. There was a large woman in a cheap dress sitting behind the desk. She pointed to the chair in front of her desk and started to speak in a groaning voice.

"Sit down Steven. My name is Kerry Shayne and I am going to be your probation officer.", looking over the desk at me, "I have spoken to your mother and stepfather and they have explained a few things to me. I am also aware of the problems that you encountered in Pennsylvania.", her voice began to get very serious, "I want you to know that I will not tolerate ANY behavioral outbursts from you. I have already made your parents aware of this. If they call me up and say that you are becoming a problem, I will not hesitate to pull you out of the house and lock you up. Do you understand me?", she shouted at me with a challenging look on her face.

"Yes Ma'am.", I answered while nodding my head, "I understand."

"Good", she smiled, "Now I just want to go over a few things with you and your parents.", She stood up and walked to the door to invite mom and David into the office.

As they took a seat, Mrs. Shayne sat on the edge of her desk and spoke to us. "Now, the three of you will probably get along just fine for the first few weeks while you get settled into life together.", she looked at us one at a time, "This is called the 'honeymoon period', and once that is over and reality sets in, there may come a point when egos start to clash.", she paused and looked directly at me before continuing her speech, "But, whatever happens, you must try to work it out. I want all of you to put forth your best efforts in trying to get along.", she looked at mom and asked, "There are two other siblings in the home, correct?",

Mom nodded, "Yes, Nicole and Robert."

"Do you get along with your brother and sister?", Mrs. Shayne asked.

"Sure, I get along fine with them.", I answered, as she looked at Mom and David, who nodded in unison.

David chimed in, "His relationship with his brother and sister is fine. That isn't what concerns me. It is his attitude toward authority that I am worried about.", he looked at me with squinted eyes. I stared back intently.

"Well, David, I am sure that the two of you as parents have had problems with Steven in the past.", she paused and looked at me, "But in his defense, I must say that it seems that the lack of proper parenting in his life has led to most of the problems that he has had. I think that as long as all of you try to get along and respect each other, everything should be fine."

"Steven, What do you think?", David asked.

"I think that she is absolutely right, David. I don't want to try to make excuses for some of the things that I have done in the past. However, I think that I am justified in saying that if I hadn't have been failed as a child, I wouldn't have had to go down the roads that went down.", I looked at him and mom, "I am not trying to lay blame here or anything. I just want to get on with my life."

Mom sat there with a blank look on her face. David looked like he was really surprised that I could make such an eloquent argument, and Mrs. Shayne just grinned. She knew that I was right. Even though she knew that I had been a troublemaker in the past, she was aware that I had gotten a raw deal in the past.

"Ok, if there's nothing else, I am going to give each of you my card.", she handed them out, "You call me if you have any problems or questions. Steven, I will be seeing you once a month. You will get a letter in the mail letting you know when your first appointment will be.", she walked us to the door and said, "Good Luck!", as we walked down the hallway.

As we were driving back to the house, there weren't many words said. David steered the car and mom just sat there looking forward. I just looked out the window and thought about seeing my brother and sister for the first time in nearly four years.

As we were approaching a convenience store, I asked if he could stop. He pulled into the parking lot and I went inside to get a pack of cigarettes. When I came out with them in my hand, they both looked at me shocked.

You smoke? How long have you been smoking?", Mom asked as I got in the car.

"A few years now Mom.", I answered

David put his hand on mom's and turned around in his seat to face me, "Look, if you smoke, then you smoke. But I don't want you smoking in the house. OK?", his voice was firm, yet sympathetic.

"Sure", I answered, "I won't smoke in the house."

"I will get you an ashtray to put outside.", he started the car and drove on, "If the weather is bad, then you can smoke in the garage, but only with the door open.", he offered.

"That will be fine.", I responded from the back seat.

He drove us home and I went and sat in the back by the pool and lit a cigarette. I looked around at the peaceful setting and felt right at home. Mom came out and sat in the chaise lounge beside me and smiled.

"I still can't believe that you smoke!", she said as she looked at me, "Did your father teach you that?", she asked. I just shrugged my shoulders.

"I don't know Mom, but it's not that big of a deal.", I answered.

"With all that you have been through, I guess that you are already sort of a grown up, huh?", she asked.

"I guess so Mom.", I smiled and leaned over to give her a kiss on the cheek, "Life hasn't been easy, but I will be OK. At least now I will be.", she smiled and held my hand.

"You will be.", she said, "You will be."

Later that afternoon, my brother and sister came home from school and welcomed me home. Nicole was now eighteen and finishing her senior year. Robert was going to be thirteen in a few months and in the eighth grade. They seemed very happy to see me. I spent a few hours with Robert going over all the stuff that had transpired since I had last seen him. He just looked at me in awe.

"Well, I am glad that you are here now!", he said as we strolled around the neighborhood.

"Me too little man, Me too!", I replied.

I spent some time with Nicole that evening and we talked about everything that was happening in my life. It was basically the same conversation that I had had with

Robert, but since Nicole was older, we spoke a lot more openly.

"Wow.", she said, "You are three years younger that me, and it seems like you have already seen and done more than I ever will!", she grabbed my hand.

"Yeah, I guess you're right, but it hasn't been easy.", I answered.

She looked at me very seriously, "You know, sometimes at night, I used to sit and cry wondering what you were going through in those places. I have always worried about you over the years.", her eyes started to tear up, "I love you brother!"

I hugged her and said, "Don't cry! I'm ok now. Look at me.", she looked in my eyes, "See, I'm ok. I made it through all of it."

She just nodded her head and cried for a minute. Getting up from the chair she said, "I'm glad that you're finally here."

"I'm glad to be here Sis!", I responded. I lit a cigarette and she gave me a devious grin, "What?", I asked as she stared, "Are you going to rag on me for smoking too?", I asked as I inhaled.

"Give me a drag you moron!", she said as she snatched from my hand and took a puff.

"What? You smoke too?", I almost shouted.

"Shhh!, she held her fingers to her mouth, "Mommy would kick my ass if she knew!"

"It's not that big of a deal.", I stated plainly.

"It is if you are teaching dance classes!", she took another hit and passed it back, "She saw a pack in my car once and freaked out. I told her that they were Marissa's!"

I just laughed and sat back on the chair. Nicole looked over at me and grinned. I guess that it did make sense that she shouldn't smoke. Mom owned a dancing school, and Nicole had been dancing since she was two years old. Now that she was older, she was teaching other kids.

Mom had decided to take a few days off of work to spend at home with me. David worked in his furniture store in North Jersey and was gone all day. I went for a little interview at my new school. Since I was transferring from another state, and the school systems were different, I already had more credits than I needed. They decided that it would be pointless for me to enroll for the last couple of weeks. I would be starting my junior year in the Fall. I had mom to keep me company during the day for a while. We would sit by the pool for hours and just talk about life and the past. She seemed surprised that I had not gone totally insane from all of the shit that I had endured. Within a few days of us hanging out, we started to grow rather close.

Mom eventually went back to work, and school ended for Nicole and Robert. I now had them to keep me company during the day. I started to make friends around the neighborhood. A few of them I had already known from the weekend and summer visits I had as a child, but it had been so long ago, it was like meeting them again.

My stepsister, Evie also joined us for the summer. Evie lived in Georgia with her mom, but usually spent her summers and Christmas breaks in NJ with our family. Evie was right in between Robert and I in age. We always got along. Even when I use to tickle torture her or hold her down and try to drip snot on her. It was all in good fun, and she was a good sport.

Summer started to pass by and toward the end I was set into my new life. Mom had just secured a new location for her dancing school and the day that we were moving stuff from the old school to the new one, David and I had our first problem.

I was backing mom's car into the garage to load some stuff into it when I heard him yelling at mom in the house. I jumped out of the car and ran upstairs to confront him.

"....you let him do whatever he wants around here. Now he is driving your car? He doesn't even have a license.", David was yelling as I ran up the stairs.

I jumped in between them and pinned him against the wall.

"What are you fucking crazy or something?", I yelled, "Don't you ever raise your voice at my mother.", staring him in the eye seriously.

"Steven, NO!", mom yelled.

"Mom, go downstairs.", I barked, I held my arm up to David and balled my fist, "I better NEVER hear you talk like that to her again!", I continued at him.

"Go ahead! Hit me!", David said, while looking at my balled fist.

I just glared at him and let him go. I stared right into his eyes. I gave him the 'Do Not Fuck With Me' look. He just stood there as I walked away and down the stairs. Mom was waiting for me near the car.

"Come on, get in!", I said to her. She got in the car on the passenger side and I drove us out of the garage. It wasn't that big of a deal to mom that I drove without a license. She knew that I could drive just fine, and sometimes she would let me drive. David had seen me backing the car into the driveway and he just let loose on her. She was sitting there as I drove. The tears in her eyes were building up.

"Mom, I'm sorry I snapped, but he shouldn't be yelling at you like that.", I said to her.

"You didn't hit him did you?", she asked.

"No, I didn't hit him. He's lucky I didn't!", I answered, "He doesn't yell at you like that a lot, does he?", I continued my questioning, "I will NOT deal with anyone yelling at you like that Mom."

"He doesn't do it a lot, but sometimes he just loses his temper.", she answered in denial like a battered woman.

"Well, those days are over Mom. I won't have it!", I said as I directed the car through traffic.

She didn't say another word about it. We went to the dancing school and began to move some furniture around. That night, when we got back, David was out somewhere. The whole ordeal faded into the background of our lives.

Summer continued in a normal fashion, and before I knew it, school was starting once again. At first, I started attending my classes on a regular basis. But after the first two months, I got extremely bored with my education. I would spend my days in school just roaming around the halls with my headphones on. If a teacher said anything to me, I would just ignore it and keep on walking. It was no surprise to me that I began to get suspended. First it was an in school suspension, which I refused to participate in. So, the school had no choice but to give me what I wanted, an out of school suspension.

I started spending more time out of school than in school. When mom and David found out that I was getting suspended, they grounded me. Being grounded in that house was not like normal grounding. I was allowed out of the house, but I had to be in by nine on the weekdays, and eleven on the weekends. To me, it was a joke. I would sometimes just not even go home for a few days at a time.

I'd go to school when I wanted, if I wanted. I just pretty much did what I wanted to do. I stopped speaking to David completely. I had no problem with mom. She and I would often talk. She knew that I was just blowing off steam sometimes. She really didn't rag on me about school. When I told her that I was concerned that David would call my probation officer and try to screw things up for me, she told me not to worry.

One night, after I had been at my girlfriend's house for about six days straight, David and I got into it again. I was about three houses down from my own, visiting with my friend Jim and his brother Tommy. They were quite aware of my situation at home with David. So, when I decided to walk down to the house to check in and see how things were going, they offered to come with me.

As I approached the house, I saw that my bedroom light was on. I climbed the porch steps and stepped onto the railing to look in the window. Jim and Tommy stood there in the grass watching. When I looked in the window, I saw David going through my dresser and stuffing my things in a plastic bag. Who the fuck did he think he was going through my stuff, I thought to myself. I climbed down, and since I didn't have a key, I rang the doorbell. David came to the door and said to me,

"What do you want?", his voice was surprisingly fierce. Mom was standing behind him looking distraught.

"What do I want? What do you think you're doing going through my stuff?", I growled.

"I'm packing up your stuff. Since you don't seem to need to stay here anymore, I figured that I would get your things together for you.", he retorted.

"Well, I am home now. So stay out of my room!", I glared at him and started to step through the door.

"You aren't coming in here!", he yelled as he slammed the door in my face. I stood there stunned. He actually slammed the door in my face. I started to kick the door. I kicked it about ten times before I gave up and turned around to head down the steps.

It was then that David burst through the door and tried to rush me. He tried to grab me, but I jumped to the side. He swung at me, and I ducked and punched him right in the face. I picked him right up off of his feet and slammed him onto the concrete porch.

"You try to hit me…", as I kneeled on his chest, continuing to punch him, "I told you not to fuck with me old man!:, I just kept on hitting him. Mom was screaming at me from the doorway for me to stop.

Jim and Tommy had seen everything and they ran up the stairs to break it up between us. As Jim began to pull me off, David yelled, "Don't try it!", and decked Jim in the mouth. Jim hit him back and yelled,

"What are you, nuts?", he was holding David by his shirt. Tommy was holding me as I struggled to get back at David. Jim went on to yell at David, "Why did you hit me?"

"You were trying to jump on me too!", David answered. His glasses were broken and hanging off his face, blood dripping from the bridge of his nose.

"You fucking idiot! Do you really think that he needed our help to kick the shit out of you? He was doing that just fine on his own.", Jim yelled as he let him go, "We were trying to break it up. What the hell is wrong with you anyway? You don't attack your own kid!", he continued to yell.

"He's not my kid! I'm calling the cops!", David yelled as Tommy walked me down the street, trying to calm me down.

"I'm going to jail dude.", I said to Jim as he caught up to us.

"He's not going to call the cops. Your mom was yelling at him that she didn't want him to call the cops as I was walking down the stairs. Just relax man. You can crash at our house tonight.", Jim put his arm around my shoulder and walked me into the house.

I was extremely stressed out. Jim and Tommy were laughing on the couch about the beating that I had just given when I saw the flashing lights go down the street.

"Oh shit, the cops are going to my house!", I yelled out, "I'm going to fucking jail for assault.", Jim and Tommy went around the back of their house to see what was happening. They came back in and told me that the cop car pulled into my driveway and one of the cops rang my doorbell. My mom came out and said a few words to him, and the cop got back in the car and drove away. About a minute later, the phone rang and Jim answered.

"Hello…yeah he's ok…uh-huh…yeah sure…I'll tell him…ok…thanks for calling. Sorry about that…Ok, goodbye.", he then hung up the phone.

"Dude, that was your mom. Apparently the people across the street called the cops, but she told them everything was fine. She said not to worry. Just try to stay away for a few days and she'd take care of David., Jim explained.

"Damn, that was close.", I said as I cracked my knuckles and started to laugh, "Did you see me kick his ass!?", I yelled.

They just started to laugh. Tommy jumped up and imitated David on the ground and Jim jumped on him. Tommy was yelling, "No Steve, don't kick my ass, No please don't beat me up! No… Help!", They went on for a few minutes. I laughed along, but I really didn't feel good about kicking a fifty year old man's ass.

A few days later, I went back home. David and I tried our best to stay away from each other. Nothing was ever said about the fight. Within a month after that incident, mom told me that her and David were getting a divorce. I asked her if it was my fault that they were splitting up and she looked at me and said,

"No, it's not your fault Steven. I am just not in love with him anymore! That is it.", her voice was one of a strong and determined woman.

"Are you sure Mom?", I asked.

"Yeah, we've been married for almost ten years. I'm just not happy anymore Son.", she assured me.

That was the plan. They were getting divorced. The house was being sold and they'd split the money down the middle. Obviously, us kids were going to stay with mom. I saw David the following day and he just looked defeated in every aspect of life. I almost felt sorry for him. I really shouldn't paint him like he was a bad man because he wasn't. He was basically an all around good guy. I just didn't get along with him. I never had. I knew that he loved my mother, and that he loved Nicole and Robert as if they were his own. I suspected that even though the two of us had our differences, he loved me too, even if it was just because I was my mother's son.

The house went on the market, and two months later, on the eve of my sixteenth birthday, Mom, Nicole, Robert and I moved into a little condo in Brick. Just a few miles down the road. I continued to attend the same school, when I actually felt like going. Robert also stayed in his school. We were now in a different school district, but we were close enough to be able to get to school. David was still living in the house, until it was sold, so according to the school, we still lived there.

Our new condo was smaller than the old house. Robert and I had to share a room. That wasn't much of a problem for either of us. I was rarely there anyhow. I had met a new girl named Renee, and the two of us were spending most of our time together.

Renee was seventeen. I was sixteen, but she thought I was a year older. She went to school in Brick, and since she had her own car, she would pick me up in the morning and drive to her school to drop her off. I would take her car all day and pick her up when her day was done. Even if I did go to school, I never stayed a full day, so I would always be available to pick her up.

On Christmas, Mom and us kids went up to Hillside to spend the day with my grandparents. While we were driving up there, I suggested that we stop at Nanny's house to see if she knew where our father was. I was driving the car, and I knew where she lived. When I made the suggestion, mom started to laugh.

"Can you imagine the look on her face if she saw all three of you kids standing on her doorstep. How long has it been since you kids have seen her?", she asked.

"The last time we saw her was when Steven came back from California, that was, what…six years ago?", Nicole answered from the back seat.

"I last saw her back in '87, before I went to Brisbane.", I stated as I drove the car.

"So, do you think we should go?", Nicole asked.

"I do, I really do! At least to see her reaction. Maybe we can find out where your father is, so I can get some of the child support he owes me.", Mom answered.

"So, I guess we're going.", I said. I drove us all the way to Linden. When I pulled up in front of the house, we all got out and walked up to the front door. Everyone looked at me. I shrugged my shoulders, and rang the doorbell. I too, was curious about what her reaction would be when she answered the door and saw her three long lost grandchildren and ex-daughter-in-law standing there on her doorstep. There was a rustle of feet coming down the steps. Then the door opened and our Nanny looked at us in utter surprise.

"Oh my God. What are you guys doing here?", she said in shock. She looked very old standing there in her housecoat.

"Surprise!", I said, "We were in the neighborhood and decided to stop by."

"Hi Nanny!", Robert said.

"Hi Robert. Look at you! You got so big.", she exclaimed, "Nicole, you're all grown up!"

She gave us each a hug and looked at mom, "Connie, how are you?", she asked.

"I'm fine Florence, how are you?", mom answered kindly.

"Well, I'm getting by.", she put her arms in the air, "Why don't you all come in? Do you have time for a cup of coffee or something?", she asked.

"Sure", I said, " Let's go inside for a cup of coffee!", directing everyone up the stairs.

We walked into the kitchen and Nanny put on a pot of coffee for us. She made a quick attempt to tidy up the table for us , but thought better of it.

"Why don't we go into the living room and sit down?", she said as she directed us to the couch. Everyone sat down but me. I just stood next to the arm of the chair next to mom.

"So, Steven, are you living with your mother now?", Nanny asked as she looked at us.

"Yeah, I have been home for about seven months.", I answered.

"And Nicole, are you done with school now?", Nanny asked.

Nicole nodded and said, "Yeah I graduated in June."

"Robert, what grade are you in now?", she continued her questions around the room.

"I'm in the eighth grade now.", Robert answered quietly.

We all just sat there quiet for a few minutes and weren't sure what to say next. Mom chimed in just in time to break the uncomfortable silence.

"So, Florence, how are things going for you?", she asked, "Is your health ok?"

"Oh, I'm ok, I guess. I retired a few years ago.", she said to mom calmly, "How are Phil and Rebecca?", referring to mom's parents.

"They're ok. My mother is well, but Dad is suffering Alzheimers, so that is hard.", she answered.

"That is rough.", Nanny stated with compassion, "Are you guys going to see them now?"

"Yes, we are having dinner there.", I answered. Nicole and Robert just sort of sat there with blank looks on their faces. They hadn't seen this woman in years, so they didn't know what to say to her. Mom gave me the look to say that she was ready to leave. I opened my eyes wide to her. I was having too much fun seeing my Nanny sweat. I looked at her and blurted out,

"Do you have any idea where my dad is?", looking intently into her eyes.

"No, I haven't seen or heard from your father in a few years.", she answered in a panic. I knew she was lying. I had seen the Christmas cards on the mantle with his all too familiar handwriting on them. 'To Mom, Love Robert and Rita', one of them was signed.

"Can I use your bathroom Nanny?", I asked.

"Sure honey, you remember where it is, don't you?", she pointed out toward the kitchen.

"Yeah, I remember.", I said as I walked out of the living room. As I was walking through the kitchen, I spied Nanny's address book sitting on the counter. I looked back to see if she could see me, and when I saw that she couldn't, I stuffed it into my pants. I went into the bathroom and opened the book. I easily found dad's number and address. I put the book back in my pants, flushed the toilet and walked back into the living room.

I gave my mom a small wink, and she stood up and said,

"Well, Florence, we should probably be going. I don't want to keep my parents waiting. You know how people can worry."

"Yeah, sure I know.", Nanny stood up as we headed out of the living room. She gave all of us a hug and a kiss on the cheek., "You kids keep in touch, ok?"

"Sure Nanny, we will. It was nice to see you!", Nicole said as we walked down the stairs.

"Bye Nanny", Robert said.

I stood at the top of the stairs with her for a second, and gave her a kiss on the cheek, "Take care.", I said as I stepped down, "It was nice to see you again."

"Stay good Steven.", she said as I walked out the door and onto the porch. Everyone was standing by the car waiting for me, since I had the keys. I opened the door and we got in. As I drove down the street, mom looked over at me,

"Do you think she was telling the truth about your father?", she asked naively.

"No, I KNOW that she was lying!", I said as I pulled up to a red light.

"How do you know? I mean, how can you be sure?", mom said.

"Well, first of all there were Christmas cards on the mantle with his handwriting on them.", I said as I reached down my pants to pull out the address book, "and then there is this!", I held it up.

"Oh my God, you took her phone book!?", mom started to snort and cackle.

I handed it to her, "His address and phone number are listed under 'R'!, I said. Mom was still laughing. Nicole and Robert were also laughing in the back seat. I felt that

I had accomplished something for my family. When mom stopped laughing, she said to me,

"What do you think she'll do?", she asked.

"What can she do? She probably went to call him the minute we pulled away. Hopefully she knows the number by heart!", I answered.

"Look, there is a listing for 'Bob Work', Mom said as she pointed in the book.

"Good, now you take that number and call it to find out where he works, so you can get him for the child support he owes you for Nicole and Robert.", I thought for a second and added, "Shit, now you can make him pay for me too!"

"Yeah, you're right.", Mom said. I looked in the rearview mirror and saw that Nicole and Robert looked a little troubled in the back.

"Are you guys ok?", I asked with concern.

"It was just weird to see her after so long, and the fact that she lied to us pisses me off!", Nicole answered. Robert just sat there with a dazed look.

"How about you little bro? Are you ok?", I asked while looking him eye to eye through the rearview.

"Yeah, I'm ok, it's like Nicole said, it was weird.", he answered.

As for me, I was fine. Actually, I felt kind of victorious. I had grown used to dad not being in my life. What once harbored in my guts as sadness, was now a ball of hate. I really didn't care either way about him. I did care though, about him paying my mother what he owed her for all the years that she took on the financial responsibility for my siblings.

We made it to my Grandparent's house and sat down for a nice dinner. Mama and Papa, as we referred to them, were happy to see all of us getting along so well. Mom told Mama about our little side trip, and about me getting the phone book.

"Good for you Steven!", she looked over at mom and said, "Now you can make the bastard pay the money he owes."

We ate the rest of our dinner without another word about our father. Later that evening, after opening gifts, the four of us went back home. It turned out to be a productive day.

Before I knew it, 1992 had rung in, and I was spending less and less time at both home and school. I would stay at Renee's house most of the time. Occasionally, I would go back to the house for a change of clothes. I rarely stayed long though.

Mom and I started to grow apart, and one day when I was at the house to pick up some things, she confronted me about my lifestyle.

"What are you doing with yourself Steven?", she asked.

I just rolled my eyes, "What Mom, what is the problem?", I responded.

She glared at me for a second and let out, "First of all, when was the last time you were in school? Second of all, where are you sleeping every night?"

"I don't have time for this right now Mom.", I stepped toward the door to escape the confrontation, but she stepped right in front of me.

"Listen, I know that you are growing up, and I can appreciate that you have a girlfriend that you want to spend time with.", she paused for a moment and continued, "But if you are going to be living here in my house, then you have to respect me. I want you to start going to school, and I want you to start sleeping here.", she looked at me seriously, "If you aren't going to live by my rules, then you aren't going to be living in my house. The choice is yours."

"Well, Mom, I guess that I am going to have to move out then, because I don't need someone watching over my every move. I am a big boy, and I can take care of myself!", I said as I stepped around her and opened the door.

I walked outside and looked back, "I will be back for my things in a day or two." I got into Renee's car and back out and drove off leaving mom standing there in the doorway.

I had come so far with my life, and now I felt like I was old enough to make my own decisions. I wasn't really getting into any trouble, so why was Mom bothering me about this and that. I figured that she would be happy that I was out of her hair. She was just concerned about me though.

I was blind to her concern. I took it as an act of dominance. As it turned out, her concerns were quite valid. In the second week of February, I was caught in the winds of a shitstorm that would prove to be worse than the others I had seen before.

THE WINDS OF THE ONCOMING STORM: HOWELL & BRICK, NJ FEBRUARY 1992

I had been out of mom's house for about two weeks when she called me at Renee's to ask me if I would come to the house to have a talk with her. Although I really didn't want to, I went anyway. When I walked in the door, mom and David were sitting in the living room waiting for me.

"Steven, have a seat.", mom pointed to the couch.

I looked at David and back at mom and said,

"What is he doing here?"

"We just need to talk to you about a few things Steven.", he interjected, "Your mother asked me to come and join her."

"So, What's up?", I said as I slouched down on the couch.

"We have spoken to your probation officer and she is aware that you are no longer living here.", mom stated, "She had suggested that we go and get some family counseling. There is an appointment for us tomorrow at ten in the morning and I really would appreciate it if you'd go.", the look on her face was one of complete worry.

"I don't know Mom, I don't like the sound of the whole thing. How can I be assured that she won't be waiting there to lock me up?", I asked.

"That isn't what this is about!", David stated, "We are trying to help you get your act together at home so you don't wind up getting yourself locked up again."

I glared at him, "First of all, I don't even understand what any of this has to do with you David. This is between me and my mother.", I barked.

"Fine, you know what, you do what you want!", David responded, "But you will not like the results!", with that said, he walked into the kitchen to leave me and mom alone.

"Steven, I am asking you to please do this.", mom said softly, "Please!"

"Ok, fine Mom, I'll go.", I said in defeat. I figured that I'd placate her emotions for the time being. I had no real intention of actually going though. "Where is the appointment at?", I asked.

"Aren't you going to go with me?", she said.

"No Mom, I will meet you there!", my voice showed my annoyance.

"Are you going to school tomorrow?", she asked.

"I don't know Mom, I guess. Why?", I answered.

"Well, maybe it would be best If I just picked you up from school?", she looked right into my eyes.

"Fine, pick me up out front at nine thirty.", I said.

"Ok, are you going to stay here tonight?"

"No Mom, I will be at Renee's. I've got her car right now, so I gotta go.", I got up and walked out of the house.

The next morning, I went to school as planned, but left shortly before nine. I didn't want to be around when mom and David showed up to pick me up. I went back to Renee's and waited until it was time to pick her up from school.

Mom called Renee's later in the morning, but I didn't answer the phone. I just let her talk to the machine. I felt bad about making her go through the task of coming to pick me up only to find that I wasn't there. I just couldn't go through with what they were asking of me. I felt a strong feeling in my gut that I wouldn't be coming back from that meeting if I had gone. I was feeling that I'd had before many, many times, so I always took heed to it.

A few days later my feelings rang true. I was pulled over driving Renee's car and taken to the police station. I had no license, and the cops were looking for me because my mom called my probation officer and she reported me as a runaway, and she issued a warrant for me for not complying with the conditions of my probation. The police didn't take me to a detention center though, they took me to a juvenile shelter instead. My probation officer had decided that it would be best for me to try to fix the problems with my mom, rather than lock me up.

I didn't give her suggestion a chance though. I ran from the place the first night and began to slink around my old neighborhood. Crashing at friends' houses here and there. Renee had gotten a phone call at school to say that her car was being impounded for being driven by a non-licensed driver. They also informed her that I was only sixteen. Needless to say, she wanted nothing to do with me after that.

Shortly after my escape from the shelter, I was arrested for criminal trespassing for going into someone's house without their permission. They would have charged me with breaking and entering. Since I had previously been friends with the kid who lived there, I knew where the key was. I told the police that I needed somewhere warm to go. In reality, I was searching through the house for some money to take.

I was taken to the Monmouth County Juvenile Detention Center to be held while a determination was made about what to do with me. When they realized that mom had moved to Brick, which was in Ocean County, I was transferred to the Ocean County Juvenile Detention Center.

OCEAN COUNTY JUVENILE COURT: TOMS RIVER, NJ MARCH 1992

There I was. Locked up again. I knew that I had no one to blame by myself this time. I was given a chance. Then another chance, and yet another. Still, the monster that had seemed to rage within my soul showed his evil face again. I went before a judge and it was determined that the court needed time to effectively review my case and background before making a determination in my case. In the meantime, they felt that I didn't need to be in the detention center. My mother was asked if she would take me back home, and she said no. So I was placed in the Ocean County Juvenile Shelter until it was decided what should be done with me.

Immediately after my arrival there, I felt flighty. I had to get out of there and fast. I called my friend Noel and had him pick me up late one night. He drove me to his house and gave me as much money as he could. He made arrangements for me to go and stay with his cousin in Staten Island, NY. I had him drop me off near my mother's condo. I took her car from the parking lot and jumped on the Parkway heading to NY. I still had my own key from when I used to drive it.

An hour later, I was crossing the bridge to Staten Island. Once again, I was a fugitive. I knew that it would be hours before mom woke up and realized that her car was missing. She might even hear that I was missing before she realized the car was gone. I doubted that she would call the police about it. She would have to realize that I was the one who took it. I knew that she would be pissed, but it didn't matter to me. I felt like I had no other choice but to leave. I figured that I could survive on my own until I was eighteen. Even though that was nearly two years away. I decided to lay low in Staten Island until I could get away somewhere else. I made plans in my head for my big, new lifestyle. But like everything else in my life, I would wind up screwing that up too.

THE REALITY OF NEW YORK WHEN YOU'RE SIXTEEN: MARCH 1992

I stayed at Kenny's house in Staten Island for about three weeks before I moved on to stay with someone else in The Bronx. This turned out to be the worst move of all for me. I was still driving mom's stolen car. I wasn't sure if anyone was looking for it or not, but driving a car with Jersey plates in New York was very common, so I blended right in. I called Christine in Erie, and told her that I was going to drive out and see her. She was under the assumption that I was still with my mother, so she welcomed my visit.

On the day that I was supposed to leave for the long drive to Western Pennsylvania, I got into a beef with someone from the neighborhood, and it resulted in my arrest. I wasn't being arrested for the car though. Somehow, it had slipped by the cops that I was driving this expensive sports car with Jersey plates. I was taken in for the altercation, and it was discovered that I was wanted in New Jersey.

I spent about six weeks in the Rikers Island Correctional Institution. Rikers was one of the largest and toughest jails in the country. The difference between the justice systems in New York and other places around the country, is that once you are sixteen years old, there are no more 'Juvenile Detention' centers. You go to JAIL! You go where the adults go. Rikers was one of the worst experiences that I had ever had in my entire life.

Out of the six weeks that I was there, I spent at least three of them fighting most of the time. It was a very dangerous place. The building that I was in, C-74 was mainly for adolescents ranging from sixteen to twenty five. The inmates there did not play games. If you didn't stand up like a man and fight, then you were weak. If you were weak, then it could mean very bad things for you. It was a common thing to see people get their faces slashed open by razor blades. From the very start, I made it a point to not to back down from anything that came my way. I fought, I fought and I fought some more. After about three weeks though, I was accepted into the inmate ranks and my problems ceased.

By the time I was transported back to New Jersey, I was exhausted. Both mentally and physically exhausted. I came through that place with barely a scratch, and I was determined to NEVER wind up in a place like that again.

I was returned to the detention center in Ocean County and locked back up. I wasn't sure what would be done to me for this latest incident, but I guessed that it wouldn't be good.

BACK IN OCEAN COUNTY: TOMS RIVER, NJ MAY 1992

Like most of my assumptions in life in the past. My assumption that I would be dealt with harshly for my absconding from the shelter and getting locked up in a New York prison was wrong.

A few weeks after I got to the detention center, I was once again sent back to the shelter. A few days later, I took off again. This time I decided to lay low locally rather than steal a car and take off.

A few weeks later, I was caught again. Once again, I was taken back to the detention center. This process continued throughout the summer of 1992. I would bounce back and forth between detention, the shelter, and being on the run. I must have ran from the place five times before the court realized that I wasn't going to stop running. To me, it didn't seem like there were any consequences for my running, so I just kept on doing it. At the end of August, I was put back in the detention center for the last time.

Finally, the court got fed up with me. The judge decided that I needed a more secure environment. He sentenced me to one year at the New Jersey Training School for Boys, more commonly known as simply Jamesburg.

Jamesburg had been a notorious institution in New Jersey for decades. If you wound up going to Jamesburg, you knew that you were at the end of your rope. This place was the last stop before you were sent to prison. I had worn out my welcome in yet another county's court, and this time, they would make sure that I was punished for my deeds.

NEW JERSEY TRAINING SCHOOL FOR BOYS: JAMESBURG, NJ NOVEMBER 1992

Jamesburg was basically a reform school. Located in the center of a large farming region, pretty much in the middle of nowhere. The grounds somewhat resembled a large boarding school. But the reality is that it was more like a school for gladiators, holding the worst of the worst of New Jersey's wayward children. Jamesburg was a juvenile prison.

The administration of the school was under the blanket of NJ's Department of Corrections. Just like adults were sentenced to state prisons, kids were sentenced to Jamesburg.

Upon entering the institution you were issued an inmate ID number, and just like the adult prison system, you were an inmate. The state's parole board were the only people that could release you once you served enough time. You were eligible for parole after serving one third of your sentence. For me, that meant that I could be released after serving only four months.

There was no fence around the place, but it was far enough out there that it would be extremely hard to run from. There were corrections officers posted at various points around the grounds, and a roving van patrol around the perimeter of the institution. You would be a fool to try and run.

Unlike other juvenile placements, Jamesburg had a large number of people over the age of eighteen. At the time, if a judge sentenced you to twenty five years as a juvenile, and you were only fifteen at the time, you went to Jamesburg.

Nowadays, the courts will just sentence you as an adult and send you to a state prison. Back then it was done differently. As a matter of a fact, if you were already serving time there, even if you were as young as fifteen, you could be transferred to an adult prison without the order of a judge. If you screwed up bad enough, they could just ship you out and put you with the big boys.

Upon my admission, I was sent to the reception building. A foreboding concrete structure located in the far corner of the grounds. This building was completely locked up. Unlike the rest of the buildings, this one had a large fence around it, complete with razor wire at the top.

I was to stay there a few weeks until I was classified. Classification was a process where they gave you various psychological and educational tests and interviews to determine the best correctional plan to suit you. Jamesburg had twelve units on the grounds called 'cottages'. Each cottage was geared toward an individual specialty like: education, drug problems, sex offenders, and so on. There were also a number of outside programs that could be offered to people who had short sentences. These were basically group homes where you wouldn't be locked up, but you were still under the blanket of the state. Halfway houses if you will.

I was issued my inmate identification number: 42175 and assigned to a cell. I spent the first two weeks in session after session with shrinks, counselors, and education specialists. It was determined that I would be better suited to go to an outside program, rather than stay locked up there. I was sent to cottage four for a short while, and in the first week of December, I was transferred to a group home in Newark, called 'Essex House'. Once again, I had slipped through the cracks of the system and was given a chance at something better.

ESSEX HOUSE GROUP HOME: NEWARK, NJ DECEMBER 1992

If Jamesburg was a juvenile prison, then this place was like Club Med. It was located right in the center of Newark on North Broad Street. There were only about ten other kids there and since we were all given a chance to avoid the perils of a place like Jamesburg, we all got along pretty well.

Some of the other kids were from Newark, and they attended their own local high schools. The other kids were taught in a classroom in the building. I was in a different situation though.

Earlier that year, during the brief period that I was actually behaving in the detention center, I had taken the GED test and received my diploma. Because of that, I was offered the chance to enroll at Essex County Community College to further my studies.

I spent the first few weeks at Essex House going back and forth to the college making the necessary arrangements to start classes in January. I took an entrance exam and started to review the classes offered to determine a field of study. My seventeenth birthday came and went, and I finally got my drivers license. As Christmas was approaching, I spoke to my mother and made plans to join her, Nicole and Robert at Mama's house for the day. Mama only lived about ten minutes from where I was at, so it was no problem for me to go.

Mom picked me up and we went to have our holiday together. After dinner, I went back down the shore with mom to get some of my clothes from her house. I took the train back to Newark, and was back at Essex House by midnight. It was nice to have some of the freedom back that I had lost by being locked up. I was now almost an adult and I was about to start college. I felt like I was on my way to making something of myself.

New Year's came and went, and it was now 1993. I had to get a few hundred dollars from Mama for books that I needed for school. She was happy to help me out since it seemed like I was finally doing something positive with my life. But, just like everything else thus far in my world, I found a way to screw it up.

The day I went to enroll and get my books, I looked at the money in my hand and instead of using it for school, I decided to get on a train and head South toward the shore.

Once again I was a fugitive. Only this time I was on the run from the state. Although I had been in Essex House, I was still an inmate. I was just serving my sentence somewhere other than Jamesburg. This meant that they would be out looking for me, just like they look for someone who escapes from a real prison.

I cautiously made my way to the area where my mother lived. I actually spent the first night sleeping in my brother's closet. My mom had no idea that I was there though. The authorities had come to the house to see if anyone had heard from me. My mother told them she had no idea where I was, so they left without any further inspection or questions.

A few days later, after roaming around and realizing that I had nowhere to go, I decided to call a police officer I had known for years for some guidance. Chris Hill, an officer with the Howell Township Police Department, had been one of my counselors when I was in Brisbane, and he had helped me out of a few issues throughout my teens. I trusted him, and his advice.

He assured me that he wouldn't just simply arrest me and drag me away. He asked me to meet him in a local pizzeria so we could talk and figure out the best way to handle my situation. After meeting him and talking everything out, he convinced me that it would be best to turn myself in. He made some calls and drove me to the police station to await transfer back to Jamesburg to continue my sentence.

SERVING THE REST OF MY SENTENCE: JAMESBURG, NJ FEBRUARY 1992

If I would have actually escaped from Jamesburg, I could have had a few years added to my sentence. But, since I had run from a program facility, I was instead charged with breach of contract and sentenced to thirty days in the 'hole'; ie, Solitary Confinement.

After my thirty days were up, I was sent to Cottage Twelve. As soon as I walked in the front door of the cottage, the other kids knew that I was not fresh into the system there. Normally, when you first come into Jamesburg, you are required to wear a state issued khaki uniform until you can have your own personal clothes sent from home. If you were a parole violator, or brought back from a program, you kept the 'Street Clothes' that you were wearing upon your arrest. Since I was wearing my street clothes it was obvious that I had been through the basics before.

The cottage was like a large brick house. On the ground floor, on one side was a large dormitory with almost 40 sets of steel bunk beds with metal footlockers welded to the ends of them. It resembled an army barracks. On the other side of the building was a small day room, and a few offices. The basement contained a large shower room with shower heads staggered across the wall, a bathroom with a long row of sinks on one side and toilets down the other. The toilets were separated with stall walls, but no stall doors.

There was also a large open area that we referred to as 'Big Deck". Big deck was where kids would go and fight out their differences. It was an everyday thing to see a circle of kids with a few fighting it out in the middle. If someone called you out to go down to Big Deck, you had better go and fight. If you didn't, there was a very good chance you would be dragged down there and get the shit kicked out of you by a bunch of kids. The guards never went down there, and they all knew what we did down there. They just looked the other way.

I walked into the dormitory and headed toward the bunk that I was assigned to. All of the eyes in the dorm were watching me. I lacked the normal bag of supplies that inmates were issued upon arrival since I had been returned from the street. So, I was without a change of clothes or hygiene supplies, or cigarettes. As I started to make up my bunk, a tall kid with a ponytail walked toward me with a paper bag in his hand.

"Hey man, you just get sent back?", he asked.

"Yeah, I ran from Essex House.", I said in my cool voice, "But I got caught and they sent me back!"

"Do you smoke?", he asked as he pulled a pack of cigarettes from his pocket and offered me one.

"Yeah, thanks!", I said as I took the cigarette and lit it, "I just got out of the hole, I really need this!", I said as I took a long drag.

"Look man, my name is Zule.", he said as he held out his hand, "Where are you from bro?"

"Steve, I'm from Ocean County.", I shook his hand in return, "Good to meet you Zule, where are you from?", I asked.

"Belmar! Do you know where that is?", he asked.

"Yeah, sure man, Monmouth County. I actually used to live in Bradley Beach, right next door to you.", I answered with a smile.

He put the paper sack on my bed and looked at me very seriously, "Look, I know how it can be to be stuck here with nothing, so here are a few things to hold you over until you get on your feet.", Zule said as he pointed to the sack.

I looked at him curiously for a moment. Was he trying to play me? Was he trying to set me up? I decided that I would test him to see if he was. After some of the things that I had seen in Rikers Island, I didn't want to start off on the wrong foot in this place.

"Listen dude, I ain't some bitch in here! If you think you can try to set me up for some crazy shit, you got the wrong one man.", I barked while staring him in the eye, "I ain't got no problem putting my hands up!"

He sneered, "Ok, man calm down! I'm not trying to pull anything. You just looked like a cool dude, and I was trying to help you out..", he looked me in the eyes and continued, "Someone said that they recognized you from the county and said that you were alright, so I decided to help you out man", he threw his shoulders back and continued, "But, if you don't need any help, then fine.", as he started to walk off.

"Hey, wait a minute.", I grabbed his arm, "Who said that they knew me?", I asked.

"Jose over there.",he said as he pointed to a kid on the other side of the dorm, who nodded at me. I remembered him from detention.

I felt like an idiot. "Look man, I'm sorry about that. I thought that maybe you were trying to make a play for me or something!", I said as I held out my hand in peace.

He shook my hand, "Don't worry about it man. It happens. It's good that you are careful like that!", he pointed to the bag and continued, "Get yourself set up and I will see if I can get you some clothes."

I opened the bag to see a carton of cigarettes, and some badly needed cosmetic items like soap, toothpaste, shampoo and deodorant. There was also a new padlock for my footlocker, which was a very necessary item to have to prevent someone from stealing your stuff.

After I got myself situated in my bunk, Zule gave me some clothes to wear, introduced me around, and even got me stoned. He broke down to me who and what to avoid. He gave me the rundown on the entire place. We quickly became friends and spent the majority of our time hanging out together. It was very easy to get drugs there, so Zule and I would spend the majority of our time stoned on whatever we could get our hands on.

The normal daily routine for us was to spend half of the day in school, and the other half working to learn a trade. Since I already had my diploma, I got to spend all day working. I chose the Audio-Video department and spent my days filming and editing. The AV department didi all of the state's training and informational videos. I quickly learned how to film and edit. I actually excelled at it quite well. There was a radio station on the grounds for the inmates to listen to. I began to learn the basics of broadcasting. Since Zule was also a high school graduate, he got a job in AV with me. We would clown around most of the time, but we did the work that we had to do with ease, so the bosses didn't mind if we screwed off when we were done.

Zule was already eighteen and serving a two year sentence for drugs. He only had a few months to go when I met him. He was also a bit of a drug addict, so whenever there was a chance to get high, he took it. I usually took it with him. It would be common for us to go through ten hits of acid in a day between the two of us. We'd get pot and smoke it like it was going out of style. Sometimes, when there was shortage of real drugs, we would inhale the aerosol from cans of air freshener just to get a buzz. Most of my individual memories from Jamesburg are a blur. I took every chance that I could to mentally escape.

I got involved in something called 'Project Option' after a few months there. Project Option was like a 'Scared Straight' program for kids in the state. Busloads of kids would be brought to Jamesburg to see what would happen to them if they screwed up in the world. We would take them around the grounds and show them what it was like to be locked up. The first part of the tour usually consisted of us yelling and screaming at them to show the mentality of the inmates. After we showed them everything, we would sit down in a conference room and answer questions about our lives and mistakes to try to help them from making the same ones. I enjoyed helping out the younger generation with things like this and would often tell my own war stories about the juvenile system. By the time the kids left, there was usually no doubt that the vast majority would never return to Jamesburg as an inmate.

Months started to fly by, and before I knew it, it was June. Zule was getting home passes on weekends and now worked every evening in the kitchen of a local retirement home. He had hooked me up with a pen-pal from North Jersey who was one of his girlfriends friends.

Her name was Donna, and she shared my love of poetry and the music of The Cure. I started to pass my free time writing back and forth to her. She helped me see the more positive side of things in the world through the words she would write to me. Since Zule was gone most of the time now, and was subjected to urine testing because of his outside work, our drug use stopped. I was glad to have Donna to help keep me busy during this time.

On the second weekend of June, my mother and Robert came to visit me. Mom brought the guy that she was dating with her. His name was Mitch. I could tell right away that Mitch was a scumbag. The first time I looked into his eyes, I knew he was completely full of shit. Mom, Nicole and Robert were now living with Mitch in his townhouse in Lakewood, just a ten minute drive from where we used to live.

I could tell that he didn't like me at all when we met. It was bad enough that my relationship with mom was rocky, to say the least. But with this guy in the picture, I knew that it would get worse. I never let on to mom how I felt about him though. Instead, I just tried to enjoy my visit. When they left, I told my brother to watch out for him. Robert was on the same page as me already and told me that he didn't trust him or like him.

Zule was paroled in late June, and I told him that I would look him up when I was released in the Fall. I missed him a lot at first. Over the time that we had been locked up together, we became like brothers.

The first week of July I was called to the administration building to speak with one of the counselors. He informed me that I would be leaving Jamesburg on July 23rd. I was astounded at the news. It seemed that all of the time I had spent in and out of the detention center had been counted toward my sentence, and with all of that time credited, my sentence was soon expiring. That meant no parole for me. I would be released as a free man. No parole, no probation. Nothing.

My only concern was where I was going to go. I was only five months from being eighteen, and I did not want to spend those months in a shelter or something. I was told that DYFS would be picking me up, and it would be up to them where I went. Three weeks later, at ten in the morning, two female caseworkers from DYFS picked me up and I was finally free!

FREE AT LAST!
(WELL, ALMOST)
JULY 23, 1993

DYFS was once again in control of my life. Rather than send me to some place that they knew I would run from, they had arranged for me to go into an independent living program. I would be given my own place to stay and financial assistance for food. The problem with the program was that I couldn't start until the following week. They wanted to put me in the county shelter for the weekend.

"Absolutely not!", I said to the caseworker as she drove, "If you try to make me go there, I will walk away immediately!", my voice was one of serious determination.

"What else can we do Steven?", she asked as she drove, "It's not like you can go home to your mother's."

I thought about it as she drove and came up with an idea.

"What if I could convince my mom to take custody of me for the weekend? Could I do that instead of going to the shelter?", I asked.

"Sure, that would be fine, but how are you going to convince her of that?", she asked me.

"Just get me to a phone to call her and I will take care of the rest.", I responded.

We went to the DYFS office and I called mom at work. I told her of the situation and she said that there was no way that I could stay with her.

"Mitch would never allow it, Steven. I'm sorry but the answer is no.", she said on the phone.

"Mom, listen to me. I just need you to agree to take custody of me. I am not going to stay at your house.", I explained, "I can go and stay with a friend until I go into the program on Monday.", I figured that Zule would put me up for the weekend.

"Ok, I will do it.", she said in defeat, "Put them on the phone and I will tell them that it is ok for you to stay with me." She gave them the ok, and I had them drop me off at her house. I wanted to spend a little time with my brother before heading to Belmar to catch up with Zule.

I went to Belmar later that day and spent a few days hanging with Zule. On Monday morning, I went to meet the caseworkers for my entry into this new program in Asbury Park.

I was set up in a boarding house above the YMCA on Main Street in Asbury Park. I could come and go as I pleased. I was given a check for three hundred dollars to use for new clothes, and I had to report to see a caseworker once a week to get my fifty dollar weekly stipend for food.

I looked around at the room that I had been assigned. It was as small as a prison cell. There was a bed, a small dresser and a small closet. That was it. Down the hall was a community bathroom for me to share with the other people living there. They were all adults, living on the fringes of society. There was a payphone in the hallway for me to use, and some vending machines downstairs with snacks in them. I was free though, that is what mattered most. I decided to jump on a train and head to the boardwalk in Point Pleasant, just about twenty minutes south.

I called my brother and he took the bus out there to hang with me for the day. He was only about twenty minutes away. This became a regular thing for us. I would take the train down, and he would take the bus. We would spend all day just hanging on the boardwalk. He would take the last bus home, and I would take the last train.

After a while, as I got to know more people in Point, I stopped going back to Asbury all together. Occasionally, I would pop in and pick up something from my room and to my appointments to pick up my money. Other than that, I stayed in Point with my new found friends. It was summertime and the town was overflowing with tourists who would rent local beach houses for the summer. There was always a party to go to, or a place to hang out at. I didn't want to spend my nights in a small room that felt like a cell when I could spend it in a nice happy beach environment. Point Pleasant became my new home!

THE FREEDOMS OF BEACH LIFE: POINT PLEASANT, NJ SUMMER 1993

I met a kid named Hoey on the boardwalk one day. My brother and I were just standing around when a fight broke out nearby. I could see that the kid who was fighting was outnumbered, so I ran over and jumped into the melee to help him out. After we chased off the other kids, he held out his hand to me.

"Thanks man.", he said as we shook hands, "My name is Hoey."

"Steve", I offered as I pointed to my brother, "This here is my little brother 'Q'."

Robert had decided that he no longer wanted to be called Robert anymore, he was now simply Q.

"Nice to meet you guys! Thanks for the help back there!", he said to us.

Q just nodded to him and asked, "What was that all about?", referring to the fight.

"Oh, some dude thought I was screwing his girlfriend and decided to try to jump me with his boys!", he answered nonchalantly while grinning.

"Were you screwing her?", I asked.

"Of course I was! Why do you think they call me HOEY!?", he said and we all started to laugh really hard.

Before I knew it, I was living with Hoey and his family. Q continued to take the bus out everyday, and the three of us would just hang on the boardwalk. Hoey was a few months younger than me and was still in high school. I had told him about my past and he saw it as a badge of honor that I had made it through Jamesburg. The three of us became like brothers.

The summer flew by quickly. We stretched out each and every day until it was over. There were a lot of girls, alcohol and drugs that summer. There was also a little bit of trouble, but nothing too major.

My suspicions about mom's boyfriend Mitch proved to be true. It turned out that Mitch was a crook. His main source of income was from buying refurbished Kirby vacuum cleaners and selling them as new. He attempted to get me to sell them, and when I told him that I thought he was a piece of shit, he brushed me aside like I was the one who was a con artist. There was also a little incident that almost wound up with me kicking the shit out of him at a local bus terminal. If it hadn't been for my mother getting in between us, I would have beat him up and probably been arrested.

Summer came to an end and Hoey and my other friends went back to school. I spend most of my weekdays just hanging around waiting for them to get out of class. A guy named Mike was dating Hoey's sister Martha, and he was also out of school, so we would keep each other company during the days.

Hoey's stepfather began to get irritated with my being there and basically kicked me out of the house. I really wasn't doing anything with my life. I got a job briefly but got fed up with it quickly and quit. I began to see myself falling into the same pattern of the things that had gotten me locked up in the past. I was sleeping in empty beach houses every night. I would climb in a window or pick a lock and just crash until morning. The owners of these houses lived hours away, so it was easy to do this undetected.

I began to date a beautiful girl named Heather, and I would often hang at her house during the day while her mom was at work, and she was at school. I would shower there and eat my meals out of her fridge. Heather didn't mind helping me out. It turned out that her cousin had been in Jamesburg with me, so she understood what I was going through in life.

As the Fall pressed on, I really began to get irritated with the way that I was living. Heather and I were no longer dating, but I was still using her house during the day. During the Thanksgiving holiday break, her mom went to Mexico and took her little brother with her. So I stayed with Heather and the two of us just played house for a bit. We had Thanksgiving at her aunt's house and it was wonderful. It was during that dinner that I decided I needed to do something with my life. I was totally in love with this girl, and yet we were no longer dating. We were best friends. It became harder and harder for me to be around her without ruining our relationship by professing me true feelings for her.

I called Christine in Erie one day, and told her that I was now free and living on my own. I also explained my current situation to her. She listened to my tale and offered me a chance to get my life together.

"Listen, I just bought a house and if you want, you can move out here and live with me.", she said into the phone.

"I don't know Chris.", I said in response, "What the hell am I going to do out there?"

"Who cares! It has gotta be better than where you are right now. At the rate you are going, you are definitely going to wind up in jail!", she said sternly, "Who knows, maybe you can go to college out here. I'm sure that would be a wonderful thing for you!", she offered.

"Maybe you're right!", I said, "Would I have to pay rent or anything?", I asked.

"No, you can just help me remodel my house.", she said with a laugh.

She was right. I needed to get away from this life I was leading. She was offering me the chance that I needed to escape my wretched past and start over. I spoke into the phone,

"Let me get some money together, and I will be there in a few days", I said to her with confidence.

"Well, I have heard that one before from you, but ok. Call me when you get here!", she gave me her work number and hung up the phone.

I called my mom to let her know that I was moving to Erie to live. She really didn't seem to care either way. I got a few hundred dollars from my Mama for the bus fare and to have for expenses. She thought I was crazy for leaving Jersey, but she agreed that maybe having a chance to start over and live my life somewhere else would be good for me. Hoey and Q were convinced that I had lost my mind and made a bet that I would be back in a week. Heather really didn't understand why I wanted to leave Jersey. I don't think that she understood the depth of my feelings for her. She wished me well and made me promise to keep in touch.

On December 3, 1993 I got on the bus for the twelve hour ride to Erie. Q and Hoey were there to see me off. As the bus was traveling down the highway, I knew in my mind that I was finally free. I was going off on a journey that was completely my own from that point on. I would be eighteen in just thirteen days. Then I would be able to really start my adult life. Far from the past that had enslaved me my entire life. Far from my family and my friends. This was my life and I was going to live it my way and for nobody else but myself. I watched the miles pass by through the window while I dreamed of the new life ahead of me. My childhood was now over.

A RETROSPECTIVE ON THE PAST: DECEMBER 2022

I would love to tell you that the story you just read has a happy ending, but unfortunately it took decades to get to my own happy ending. Since getting on that bus, my trials and tribulations haven't ended. While I may have gotten my life together in certain aspects, it took me a long time to get it right.

Since the day that I arrived in Erie on that bus, I accumulated a total of three criminal cases. The first two resulted in small county jail sentences and probation. The third resulted in a seven to fourteen sentence in a state prison.

Obviously, I am to blame for the actions that landed me in prison. However, I want you to consider the following:

With all that I had to endure as a child, is it not possible that my actions throughout my childhood and young adulthood were the result of an ingrained sense of failure and lack of self worth. Could it be that I was destined to go down the path I went down. I can't blame anyone for my actions , but deep within my heart, I believe that IF I would have been given the proper love and care that a child needs, I wouldn't have done the things that I have done.

I don't want you to think for one minute that I condone any of the things that I have done in the past that have hurt others around me. I do not. I also agree with the masses that I am the master of my own future. I have been dealt with a lot in life, and I've had plenty of transgressions that I have been made to pay for. I accept the responsibility for those transgressions.

One may ask what is the real point of this book? People have asked me in the past, "Steve, who would want to read a book about your past?", or "Who cares what you went through as a child?", or even, "So many people had a rough childhood, what makes you so different?" My answer to those questions is simple: I DON"T KNOW. The truth of the matter is that I have always felt a need to share my story. If only to prove a point.

I wanted to set out to write a book about the juvenile system. A book that would illustrate all of the dangers to these children caught in a world that doesn't want them. A book that would paint an accurate picture of the hells that a lot of children go through everyday in our society.

I don't have a bunch of fancy degrees, and I am not some social worker writing a textbook. I chose to use my own story as an example of my point. After all, would you really want to read some boring textbook full of abstract facts and figures written by someone who lacked the real world experience of their topic? Or does it make more sense to take it from someone who has actually been there. To me, the latter makes the most sense.

So many of our youth today are in jeopardy. There are thousands of kids out there right now who are on the same path that I was on when I was a kid. The system continues to take children with emotional or family problems and mix them with juvenile delinquents. This practice can and usually will prove to be disastrous for those children. If you take a child who doesn't know anything, and subject him to the mentoring of a criminal, then the result you will get is most likely another criminal. A criminal bred out of what was once a troubled child.

In my case, that child had already been shown the door, so what was left? I realized when I was about fourteen that I was going to be stuck in the system until I was an adult. There was no real out for me. Sure, I was given chances, and I blew them. But what can you expect from a kid that was raised to believe that he wasn't going to amount to anything. Are the end results all that surprising?

As I type this, I am just past my 47th birthday. I have my own children, now grown, and when I think of the horrors that I saw as a child, I am thankful that my own children never had to endure anything like that.

The dissenters out there might say that myself and the rest of the kids that graduated from the juvenile system into the adult system were just plain old bad kids who got what was coming to them. That may be true in some cases. But, I have run into plenty of kids that I was put away with when I was a kid. Some of them I ran into when I was in prison. Some of them turned out to be drug addicts. Some of them are even dead. But the reality is that most of these kids just needed a stable and loving home as the root of their existence. I am sure that some of them would have grown into that they became regardless of a loving home.

Today's answer to juvenile misdeeds seems to be to just lock them up. Treat them like adults if they go out and commit adult crimes. This, in my eyes, isn't always the best practice. The reality is that sometimes kids screw up. Just because of that, they shouldn't be subjected to a world that will wind up making them worse. Sometimes kids steal money. Sometimes they steal cars. These things are nothing new to our society. They will no doubt continue throughout time. But just locking them up is not the answer. Something else needs to be done to help our youth. Unfortunately, I don't have all of the solutions. I think that family is the strongest foundation of a child's development. Love and nurturing can go a lot further than a lock and key.

Today's parents need to take more of a hand in their children's growth. If your child is in the garage making bombs after school, and you don't know about it, it is entirely your fault, as a parent, if he goes out to and decides to blow something up.

We, as a society, have opted to take the easy route by giving our kids the freedom to do whatever they want. So much so, that if they go out and do something crazy, the world asks why? If we took more time and interest in what our children were doing and supported them emotionally when they needed it, then maybe the world would grow to be a much better place.

I don't have all of the answers to fix the world. This book is not so much about the world, but the children. Specifically the children who are stuck in the juvenile system. There has got to be a better way to give these kids the support that they need to grow into productive adults. Parents who read this need to recognize that if your child makes a mistake and winds up being put away for it, the greatest thing that you as a parent can do for them is to give them the support that they need to get through those times. You need to make sure that they have a loving and supportive home to return to.

If you take a child, and give them no options, then odds are they are going to make their own. Those self made options are usually the ones that lead down a much darker path.

Some kids will just be bad. Some will just continue to be incorrigible and wind up growing up and old in a state prison. Nothing can prevent that. There will always be crime, and there will always be punishment. But, I urge all of you to try to help today's youth in every way that you can to avoid pushing them down that path. Even if it is something as simple as becoming a 'Big Brother or Big Sister', or just taking the time to help mentor a neighborhood kid who seems to be lacking structure in their own home. These things can do wonders. Every little bit can count toward making a better future for our youth. If you can help one child do something positive for their future, then you have done your part.

If you are a child reading this book, especially a child who is in one of the places like I was when I was growing up, then I want you to please, and I stress please, think about what you are doing before you do it. The path that you are taking, or thinking of taking can easily land you in prison someday. Or worse.

If you are locked up in some juvenile institution or group home, and you don't have the necessary support from your family that you need, then just try to take each day one at a time and try your best to learn as much as you can. Learn a trade, get your diploma. Don't allow the world that you have found yourself in drag you down. You can make it if you want it bad enough. Just don't give up and sell yourself short the way I did. Believe me, you won't like the end result.

Even now, decades later, I sometimes feel like none of this really happened. Like it was just a dream, or it happened to someone else. Deep down, my reality is different. When I look into the mirror, and my reflection stares back at me, the depth of my eyes tells me the real truth.

Writing this book has been one of the hardest things I have ever done. Maybe even harder than surviving the subject matter. I have had to mentally replay some horrible things in my mind, and maybe that is a good thing, or maybe it is a bad thing. But either way, I needed to do it. Hopefully, my story will help someone out there. That is all I want, nothing more.

MY FAMILY

When it comes to my family, I am sure that some of you are wondering what became of my parents or my relationship with them.

Well, my mother and I have grown quite close since the days of my youth. It was not the easiest thing to get past for either of us. She has apologized for her lack of understanding me as a kid, and openly admitted that she should have stood up and fought for me as a child. I carried a lot of angst toward her for many years as a result of my youth. However, I learned along the way that carrying that weight will only make life worse and it will literally weigh you down emotionally.

David and I are now very close. We worked past any issues we had many years ago. Although he is no longer married to my mother, he will always be a father to all of us. He is family, and nothing can change that. Him and I have had many conversations over the years about my youth, and I think that we both accept some of the blame for any failures that occurred. He really is a wonderful man. I realize that I painted him harshly throughout most of these pages, but I was merely recalling things as they happened.

As for my father, well, I haven't seen him since that day in the courthouse in 1988. My take away from that and from his absence is simple: It's his loss, not mine.

ACKNOWLEDGEMENTS

The vast majority of this book was written in 2003 while I was serving my seven to fourteen year sentence. The original manuscript was written with a typewriter and the manuscript basically sat in a box for nearly two decades.

I tried so many times over the years to sit down and retype all of it into a computer, but honestly, reliving the trauma of my childhood was too much for me. I did have a copy or two bound and let people close to me read it, and always received good reviews and so much inspiration to publish it. My problem was that I couldn't get out of my own way.

Finally, after securing a job in the mental health field and seeing firsthand what had happened to others who went through some of the same things, I decided to get out of my own way and do it.

First and foremost, I want to thank my wife Tricia for always encouraging me to be the best version of myself, and for putting up with me while I was completing this book. You have no idea what it means to me to have someone so great behind me.

My family; Mom, David, Nicole, Robert, Evie, my children, Channing and Tia, I know that I haven't always been a perfect son, sibling or father, but I want all of you to know that I love you dearly and I couldn't be the man that I am without you guys.

My nieces and nephews; Matt, Rhys, Sirran, and Livia, I love you guys and can't wait to see you all climb to the top!

Ravenis '*I-CAN-RUN-A-MARATHON*' Prime, my brother from another mother, Thank you for always believing in me and giving it to me straight! Whether I liked it or not, I always got the no holds barred opinions from you on everything, and it makes me a better man.

Momma Janet Lindsey, You always believed in me as a man and I thank you for everything you have ever done for me and other members of my family. I also thank you for giving the world such an amazing son who I will always consider a brother. Your guidance and wisdom gave him the tools to be a wonderful father to Ravi, X'Z, and Jaxon! You will be missed Momma!

Radiance Sheppard, what can I say? You put me on the path to finally get this thing to print. I will always consider you an amazing friend and I value you in my life, more than you can ever know.

Noel Jeffrey, my lifelong friend. Damn brother, we go back more than 30 years, and you were there with me through so many of the trials and tribulations contained in these pages. There will never be a day that I am not thankful for your friendship.

Melissa Bernal, your words of encouragement and support through not only reading, but finally getting this to print will never be forgotten. You have no idea how hard it was for me to hand my manuscript to an English Teacher to read. I was so scared that it would come back with a bunch of red lines all over it.

Christine Dance, although we have lost touch and went through our own issues in the past. I want you to know that I am eternally thankful for everything you did for me as a kid and a young adult. You and your entire family always welcomed me with open arms. Even when I didn't deserve it.

Glenda Shafer and family, you guys have no idea just how much you will mean to me! Glenda, I am so glad that you were there in the room the day my daughter was born!

Chris Hill, your impact on me as a young, vulnerable child has never left me. Since the day we met nearly 35 years ago. I am so thankful for everything that you did to not only try to keep me out of more trouble, but to guide me to safety more times than I can count! Thank you for all that you have done for me, and all that you continue to do for our youth! Your impact is felt by many.

Art Hilinski, If it weren't for you, I may have never made it through with my sanity. Thank you for reading my manuscript so many years ago, and believing in me enough to go to bat for me.

And for those of you that read the original manuscript and gave me encouragement to continue the path to get it published, you are not forgotten; Anissia Lahr, Katie Dick, Stephanie Karr, Maureen Androski, Sarah Shestok, Sally Barcheski, and Fakemattress; I am grateful to all of you for your support.

-Steven

For any questions, comments, bookings, or just to reach out and say Hi, I can be reached at :

steveparisbook@gmail.com

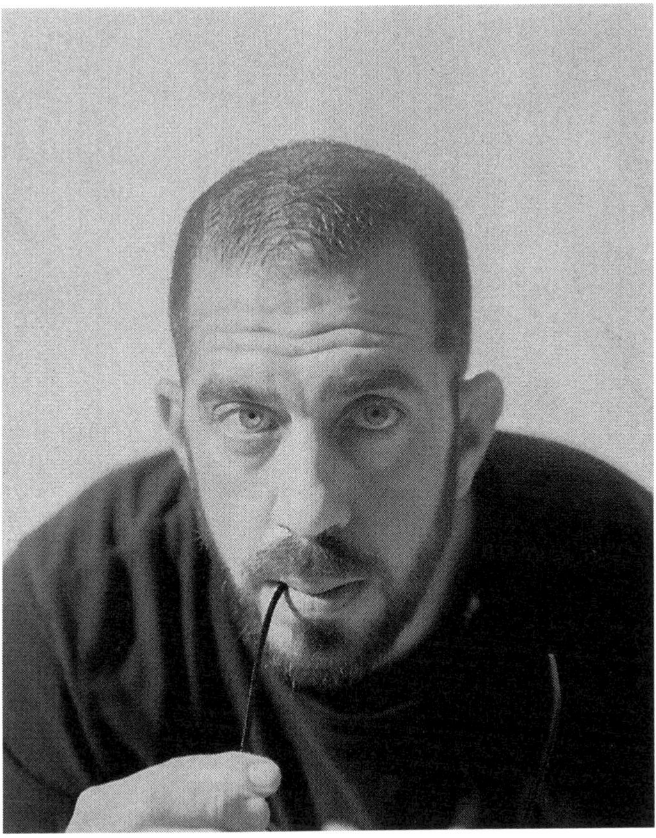

Made in the USA
Middletown, DE
03 November 2023

41823697R00187